"I was delighted to discover that Sister Kathleen had written 52 five-minute Gospel plays for education and worship. She offers catechists easily reproducible playlets for use at all grade levels. They can be incorporated into lessons on the miracles, the parables, or related topics. The stories are simple and so is the vocabulary.

"Sister Kathleen provides background scriptural information along with points for discussion, an introduction on miracles and parables in general and guidelines for putting on the plays, an index to themes and a list of Sunday Gospels about miracles and parables—all help incorporate the playlets into the curriculum and correlate their use with the liturgical year as well."

Sr. Alice Doll, OSF
St. Cloud Visitor

"Religion teachers will now be able to enliven and enrich their instruction in the New Testament by using *Acting Out the Miracles and Parables* in their classrooms. The author sees the playlets as suited to many objectives...to introduce, develop, or review a lesson...to lead into a prayer experience...to enhance a liturgical or paraliturgical service...to be shared and enjoyed by students in other classes, by parents or other groups."

The Catholic Transcript

"With the help of veteran educator and author, you can incorporate the presentation of 28 of the most memorable miracle stories and 24 of your favorite parables from the Gospels in your education classes and worship settings.

"The thematic index guides you right to the particular lesson or quality of Jesus you want to emphasize in your teaching or preaching. The worship reference guide in this practical volume directs all 52 plays to pertinent Sundays of the church year (Cycles A, B, C)."

Book World

"This is a valuable book for introducing your people to the Scriptures and the life of the church. The author has taken most of the miracles and parables from the Gospels and presented each as a drama. The playlets have simple staging instructions and there are some overall guidelines on how to use the material. Anyone teaching, or preparing liturgy with children, will find this a most useful book."

Intercom

D1361659

"This collection of original playlets grew out of Sister Glavich's experiences as a teacher....using the themes, comments, and points for discussion provided for each playlet, students can be guided through relevant and interesting learning experiences.

"Sister Glavich has also provided a Sunday Liturgy calendar with the corresponding miracle/parable themes, as well as a cross-referenced index to the themes. The book closes with a selected bibliography of works on the miracles and the parables."

Mississippi Today

"Sr. Mary Kathleen, an experienced educator, provides a special selection of miracle and parable 'playlets' for classroom or parish use (or by the resourceful parent!). Written to fill a need, it is intended to supplement an ongoing catechetical program. Included are some helpful hints about putting on playlets. The stories can readily be adapted to the ages of the children concerned. A useful resource in any teacher's religious library."

The Furrow

"These 28 miracle accounts and 24 parables of Jesus, intended as a supplement for classes, may also be used for worship services. There is a chart listing the liturgical cycle and the title of the appropriate play. A topical index lists the miracles and parables according to theme. A bibliography on miracles and parables is included. The director's handbook provides information for classroom use: themes, comments, and points for discussion. Most plays have eight principals, with extras needed for crowds. There are a number of plays that can be performed in one minute....very good for schools."

Mary Mueller
Modern Liturgy

"Sr. Mary Kathleen, a Sister of Notre Dame, has been active in religious education for over twenty years. She presents five-minute plays based on 28 miracle stories and 24 parables. There is a worship reference guide relating the plays to the Sunday readings and an index of themes."

Theology Digest

Sr. Mary Kathleen Glavich, SND

A·C·T·I·N·G O·U·T
THE MIRACLES
AND PARABLES

52 Five-Minute Plays for Education and Worship

TWENTY-THIRD PUBLICATIONS

Mystic, Connecticut

Acknowledgments

I am grateful to Sister Mary Joell Overman, S.N.D., Sister Rita Mary Harwood, S.N.D., and Sister Mary Nathan Hess, S.N.D., for their support of my writing ministry. Special thanks to Sister Mary Jane Vovk, S.N.D., and Sister Mary Donnalee Resar, S.N.D., whose enthusiasm sparked this book, to Sister Mary Renée Pastor, S.N.D., who offered suggestions for the scripts, to Sister Mary Catherine Rennecker, S.N.D., who painstakingly typed and proofread the manuscript, to Sister Mary Dolores Abood, S.N.D., who graciously did the final proofreading with an eagle eye, and to the people at Twenty-Third Publications who brought the book into being.

I also wish to express my appreciation to Reverend Lawrence Tosco, C.S.J., whose course on miracles was an inspiration and a delight.

Sixth printing 1997

Twenty-Third Publications
185 Willow Street
P.O. Box 180
Mystic, CT 06355
(860) 536-2611
800-321-0411

ISBN 0-89622-363-9
Library of Contress Catalog Number 88-50330
Printed in the U.S.A.

To the Sisters
in my community

CONTENTS

Playlets on Parables

Director's Handbook

Acting Out the Miracles and Parables

INTRODUCTION

Acting Out the Miracles and Parables: 52 Five-Minute Plays for Education and Worship has its roots in my sixth-grade CCD class. When I inherited my twenty-five rambunctious youngsters, they were accustomed to taking a fifteen-minute recess during class. This period could stretch to twenty minutes or more, depending on the amount of clothes to be put on and taken off, travel time, and the fights that broke out on the playground. To me, the minutes allotted to catechesis are far too precious and few to be spent playing. My students were not happy when I announced my no-recess policy. I mollified them by promising to plan some exciting activity for each class that would make up for their missing recess. In a short time I discovered that the students' favorite recess-substitute was performing a play.

Later that year a catechist friend asked if I knew of a book of Bible plays. With my class in mind, I had to respond, "No, but I wish I did." That was the start of this book.

Acting Out the Miracles and Parables contains twenty-eight miracle accounts and twenty-four parables of Jesus in playlet form. It is intended to supplement the regular religion program. The playlets can be incorporated into lessons on the miracles, the parables, or related topics. They are an alternative to having the students read the textbook, read the Bible, or produce their own plays. Granted that student-created plays are interesting, fun, and effective learning activities, but prepared scripts are more accurate and less time-consuming.

These brief plays can be used in the context of a lesson as

• a lively introduction
• a method of developing a Bible story
• a review activity
• a culminating activity
• a lead into a prayer experience.

They can be presented

• for another class or other group
• as part of a program for parents and other guests
• within a liturgical or paraliturgical service.

The playlets are adaptable to any grade level for several reasons. The gospel stories themselves are simple and so is their vocabulary. Most of them are familiar. Furthermore, the lessons of the basic religion text provide the necessary preparation and follow-up that make the playlets consonant with the students' developmental stage.

Most of the wording of the playlets is based on the 1986 edition of *The New American Bible*. Those playlets for miracles and parables that appear in more than one gospel account are a blend of the versions. Where dialogue is described in Scripture or merely implied, it has been supplied.

Each playlet in this book is on a separate page so that copies can be duplicated for the actors and for others connected with staging the playlets. Cast names marked + in the Director's Handbook can be adjusted to the size of the class to allow as many students as possible to participate.

Catechists, especially novice producers and directors, should not miss the feature "Tips for Putting on Playlets" on page 91. The ten suggestions there are very important for smooth performances that are rewarding for all involved.

There are two aids to help catechists plan times when the playlets would be most appropriate. For ease in preparing for Sunday liturgies that may be enhanced by a playlet, there is a chart on pages 125-126 of those Sunday gospels in each liturgical cycle which are about a miracle or a parable. To assist in correlating the playlets with the year's curriculum, a topical index is provided, which lists the miracles and parables according to theme.

The director's section of the book prepares catechists to use the playlets. Each miracle and parable is explained briefly under Comments. These notes clarify what happened, supply background information for better understanding of the event, and indicate its significance. In addition, topics for discussion are suggested for each playlet. Some of these points focus on the basic message of the Scripture passage. Others are meant to reveal the meaning of concepts that students might find puzzling or might overlook. Most important, some points lead the students to relate the events to themselves and their world.

A bibliography of readable books about miracles and parables is included for those catechists who desire to pursue the topic beyond the material in the following section, "About Miracles and Parables," and the notes for each playlet.

This book should be a help to me, to my friend, and to all catechists who regard variety and student involvement as essential ingredients of a good lesson. Its ready-made playlets will enable us to teach creatively without undue time spent preparing plays. In addition, our students will encounter Scripture and Jesus in an enjoyable way: through an experience they will remember more than reading a page in a book...or having recess!

About Miracles and Parables

Jesus attracted people by his wondrous deeds and by his teachings: "Many began to believe in his name when they saw the signs he was doing" (John 2:23). "The crowds who listened were spellbound by his teaching" (Matthew 7:28).

We meet Jesus today in the gospels. There, accounts of the miracles, his wondrous deeds, and of the parables, his teachings, touch our hearts the way they touched the hearts of people in Palestine two thousand years ago. We come to know Jesus through these stories handed down by the early church. We come to know who he is and how he thought. Knowing him, we know God; and knowing God, we have a better grasp of our own identity and destiny.

Both the miracles and the parables are mysterious. This is not surprising because Jesus himself is a mystery. Through the reflections of the disciples, theologians, and saints of the past twenty centuries and through the light of the Holy Spirit, the church has grown in her understanding of Jesus' life. By study, we share in that understanding, and by our own pondering we see more clearly the meaning certain gospel events have for us personally.

This book on miracles and parables is intended to assist you in introducing them to your students. May it also deepen your own appreciation of them and of Christ, the miracle-worker and storyteller who changed the course of history.

Miracles

In the synoptic gospels, miracles are called deeds of power. In John's gospel they are referred to as "signs." This is an apt word because it conveys the functions of miracles: They are signs of God's presence and power. In the case of Jesus, miracles are signs of the kingdom of God breaking into our world.

The prophet Isaiah in the Hebrew Scriptures described the signs that would herald the coming of God's kingdom:

Then will the eyes of the blind be opened,
the ears of the deaf be cleared;
Then will the lame leap like a stag,
then the tongue of the dumb will sing (Isaiah 35:5-6).

When John the Baptizer sent his disciples to ask Jesus, "Are you the one who is to come or should we look for another?" Jesus replied, "Go and tell John what you have seen and heard: the blind regain their sight, the lame walk, lepers are cleansed, the deaf hear, the dead are raised, the poor have the good news proclaimed to them" (Luke 7:20-22).

Jesus' message was that the reign of God was at hand. His miracles demonstrated the truth of his words. The first sign he worked, turning water into wine at a wedding feast, was a symbol of the arrival of the kingdom. The prophet Amos had described messianic times in terms of abundant wine: "The juice of grapes shall drip down the mountains, and all the hills shall run with it" (Amos 9:13). Most of the other miracles Jesus worked show power over different kinds of evil. He healed sick bodies and minds. He cast out demons. He quelled life-threatening storms. He brought the dead to life. By conquering the signs of Satan's kingdom—sin, sickness, and death—Jesus demonstrated that the reign of evil was at an end.

Clearly in Jesus God was with his people again, even more visibly than Yahweh had been with Moses and their other ancestors. God's goodness was manifest in the compassionate and loving deeds of Jesus. When the distraught leper says, "Lord, if you want to, you can heal me," Jesus replies, "Of course, I want to." When Jesus meets the widow crying over her dead son, he is moved to bring her boy back to life.

Jesus did not perform miracles like magicians who did them for popularity or profit; he didn't perform them to satisfy curiosity or even to save his life. When Herod asked him to do some tricks for entertainment, and when the Pharisees asked him for a sign, Jesus did not comply. His miracles were usually a response to someone's misery or someone's faith.

He also taught through his miracles. Those he worked on the sabbath illustrated his lesson that the sabbath was for the sake of people and not vice versa. This lesson was directed to the Pharisees, those zealous laymen who stressed the keeping of the law and its multiple prescriptions more than love of neighbor.

Especially in Mark's gospel Jesus asked those who experienced a miracle to keep it a secret. It could be that he did this to discourage people from acclaiming him as the Messiah. He was not the kind of Messiah they expected: a political savior who would overthrow Rome and establish Israel as a world power. Another explanation why Jesus kept the news of his acts quiet was that he wanted to teach us that miracles of themselves are not the important thing. In his value system, loving others, living justly, and converting one's heart surpass physical wonders.

Some people don't believe Jesus worked miracles. They think they can be explained scientifically or that the first Christians invented the stories. But most Christians realize that the burst of miracles described in the gospel cannot just be dismissed. The commentators allow for the possibility, though, that oral tradition and literary devices might have modified the original happenings. The early Christians who composed the gospels lived on the other side of Easter. As a result, their accounts of the miracles are influenced by their new insights into Jesus. According to William Barclay, these are not tall stories but deep stories.

The bottom line is that it is logical for Jesus to work miracles. In Jesus Christ God breaks through all barriers. Who would have imagined that almighty God would become a human infant, that God would die for mere creatures, or that God would remain with us in the forms of bread and wine? Yet, through Jesus, God does these wonder-full things. Other miracles are a matter of course. Furthermore, miracles are in keeping with the extraordinary mission of Jesus. He proclaims a kingdom that is here, but not yet. He overturns accepted social and religious codes. He invites people to go beyond what is normal to a new moral system, new dreams, and new hopes. In all spheres he explodes the parameters of the present reality. Little wonder then that for Jesus the impossible becomes possible.

All miracles are eclipsed by and derive meaning from Jesus' greatest sign: his resurrection. By this miracle of God raising Jesus, Jesus overcame sin, death, and all evil forever. Now he empowers his disciples to carry on his work of transforming the world and bringing about the kingdom by miracles of love and goodness.

Parables
Jesus' stories known as parables are the chief characteristic of his teaching style. The word "parable" is from the Greek for "comparison." In parables Jesus illustrates supernatural truths by means of natural images. C. H. Dodd in *The Parables of the Kingdom* offers a definition of a parable that stresses its riddle-like quality: "The parable is a metaphor or simile drawn from nature or common life, arresting the hearer by its vividness or strangeness, and leaving the mind in sufficient doubt about its precise application to tease it into active thought." In colorful English, Archibald M. Hunger's definition in *The Parables Then*

and Now pinpoints a parable's element of surprise: "one of those stories in the bible which sounds at first like a pleasant yarn, but keeps something up its sleeve which suddenly pops up and knocks you flat."

Jesus used parables to communicate the mystery of the kingdom. In them he tells about God, the kingdom of God, and the qualities expected in those who follow him. The secrets of the reign of God that Jesus tries to educate us to are so foreign and grand that he gave only glimpses of various facets: the kingdom is like a treasure, like a wedding feast, like a mustard seed. In addition, the parables show God acting in unexpected ways; they teach lessons that turn common notions upside-down.

Through parables Jesus led people gently and subtly to a new way of thinking and acting. He usually directed a parable to a certain audience, challenging hearers to take a new look at themselves and their attitudes. In some parables he explained why he associated with sinners. In other parables he stressed the urgency of repenting before the coming of the kingdom.

The parables are uncluttered with details and drawn with only the strong skeleton of a plot or a sharp characterization. In general they illustrate that our ultimate destiny depends on our response to the domestic, social, and economic setting of our lives. The parables employ simple language, ordinary objects, and familiar situations. Consequently, they charmed listeners of all ages and levels of intelligence and left a lasting impression. Their simplicity gave the parables universal appeal and made them easy to relate to. Some of them, however, are as puzzling as a Rubik's cube, especially without the knowledge of the culture which is their background. John Shea compares a parable to a joke: you either get it or you don't.

Parables have three levels of meaning: the original meaning Je-

Jesus intended, the meaning of the primitive church, and the reinterpretation of the evangelist. The early church viewed the parables in light of their own world. A few of these interpretations found their way into the gospels where the evangelists arranged them to suit their own purposes. Sometimes—especially for the sake of teaching faith or morals—a parable is treated as though it were an allegory. Every element is assigned a symbolic meaning. For example, when St. Augustine analyzed the parable of the Good Samaritan, in his eyes the victim corresponded to Adam, the thieves to the devil, oil to good hope, and the inn to the church. However, from the early days of the church, the principle guiding the interpretation of parables has been to look for one dominant point and not to be concerned about the details. We should focus our attention on our Lord's fundamental intention for telling the parable. Moreover, as we read or listen to a parable, it is good to ask what God is saying to us personally, as a community and as individuals. If we open our hearts and are responsive to his message, then we will know for ourselves how alive and transforming God's word is.

A Final Note

A bond exists between miracles and parables. Both are manifestations of the power of Jesus and his means of proclaiming the kingdom of God. But their similarity lies deeper than this. If we understand the essence of miracles and parables, we see that miracles are really parables and parables are really miracles.

Water Into Wine

John 2:1-11

(Jesus, Disciples, and Guests stand talking. Mary speaks to the Bride, and the Headwaiter to the Groom. Servants 1, 2 stand together.)

Narrator   Jesus worked the first sign of his divine power at Cana in Galilee.

Mary, Jesus and his disciples were guests at a wedding there. The servants were probably the first to realize that there was a problem.

Servant 1   The wine ran out. What can we do?

Servant 2   I don't know. How embarrassing for the family!

(Mary goes to Jesus. The Bride and Groom speak together.)

Mary   *(to Jesus)*
They have no wine.

Jesus   Woman, why turn to me? My hour has not yet come.

Mary   *(walks over to Servants)*
Do whatever he tells you.

Jesus   *(to Servants)*

Fill those jars with water.

Narrator   *(while Servants fill the jars)*

There were six stone jars standing there. The people used them for ritual washings. Each one could hold about twenty-five gallons. The servants filled them to the brim

Jesus   *(to Servants)*
Now draw out some water and take it to the headwaiter.

(Servant 1 ladles water into mug and takes it to the Headwaiter.)

Servant 1   Sir, would you taste this wine, please?

(Headwaiter takes a sip and gestures to Groom to come.)

Headwaiter   *(to Groom)*
This is delicious. People usually serve the best wine first and the cheaper wine when the guests have drunk a lot. But you have kept the best wine until now.

Disciple 1   *(to Disciple 2)*
Did you see that?

Disciple 2   I think we can believe this man Jesus.

The Calming of the Storm

Matthew 8:23-27   Mark 4:35-41   Luke 8:22-25

(Jesus and Disciples stand near boat.)

Narrator   The day had been long and busy. Jesus had preached to crowds of people. He had cured many of the sick. It was evening now and Jesus was tired.

Jesus   *(to Disciples)*
Let us go across the lake to the other side.

Disciple 1   Fine. Our boat is docked right here.

Disciple 2   Jesus, why don't you try to get some rest in the back of the boat?

Jesus   That sounds like a good idea.

(Jesus and Disciples board boat. Jesus lies in last seat with his head on cushion.)

Narrator   The Sea of Galilee was known for its sudden storms. As the disciples' boat sailed along, a strong wind arose and blew down on the lake. Huge waves broke over the boat. But Jesus was sound asleep.

(Sound of storm. Disciples rock back and forth.)

Disciple 3   We're taking in a lot of water.

Disciple 4   We can't last much longer.

(Disciples 5 and 6 stagger back to Jesus and shake him.)

Disciple 5   Master, don't you care?

Disciple 6   Save us. We're going down.

(Jesus wakes, stands, and extends his arm to the sky.)

Jesus   Quiet now. *(Extends his arm to the sea.)* Be still. *(to Disciples)* Why are you afraid? Where is your faith?

Disciple 1   *(to Disciple 2)*
Who can this be?

Disciple 3   *(to Disciple 4)*
What kind of man is this?

Disciple 5   *(to Disciple 6)*
Even the winds and the sea obey him!

The Multiplication of Loaves

Matthew 14:13-21   Mark 6:30-44   Luke 9:10-17   John 6:1-15

(Jesus is standing before the Crowd and speaking to them.)

Narrator   Jesus had gone off with his apostles so they could be by themselves and rest a little. But a large crowd had followed Jesus. He taught them and healed the sick until evening.

(Peter, Andrew, and Philip come to Jesus.)

Peter   It's very late and this is an out-of-the-way place.

Andrew   Send the people away so they can get something to eat in the village.

Jesus   They don't have to leave. Give them something to eat yourselves.

Philip   Do you want us to spend two hundred days' wages on bread to feed them all?

Jesus   How much bread do you have here?

Andrew   *(presenting Boy)*
There is a boy here who has five loaves of barley bread and two dried fish. But this will not be enough for all these people.

Jesus   *(taking bread and fish from Boy)*
Have the people sit in groups of about fifty.

(Apostles arrange Crowd in groups.)

(Jesus takes the bread and fish and looks up to heaven.)

Jesus   Thank you, Father, for the gift of this bread and fish that will feed us.

Jesus   *(handing bread and fish to the Apostles)*
Here, pass out this food to the people.

(Apostles distribute the bread and fish. The Crowd shares it. Then the Apostles join Jesus to eat.)

Narrator   All the people there, the five thousand men, the women, and the children had as much as they wanted to eat.

Jesus   *(to Apostles)*
Gather the leftovers. Let's not waste anything.

(Apostles collect pieces in baskets.)

Person 1   Look, they have filled twelve baskets.

Person 2   Surely this is the Prophet who is to come into the world.

The Large Catch of Fish
Luke 5:1-11

(Simon Peter, Andrew, and Partner are by one boat. James and John are by the other. They are washing the nets. Jesus, near Simon Peter's boat, speaks to Crowd, which is pushing to get closer to him.)

Narrator	One day Jesus spoke to a crowd of people on the shore of Lake Gennesaret.
Jesus	The kingdom of God is upon you.
Person 1	What did he say?
Person 2	I don't know. There are too many people around him.

(Jesus gets into nearest boat and sits down.)

Jesus	Simon, would you please push off a little distance from the shore.

(Simon, Andrew, and Partner enter the boat and row.)

Narrator	Jesus taught the crowd from Simon's boat. When he finished, he spoke to Simon.
Jesus	Simon, go out further to the deep water and lower your nets for a catch.
Simon	Master, we have worked hard all night long and have caught nothing. But if you say so, I will lower the nets.

(Simon, Andrew, and Partner let down nets.)

Simon	Look at all the fish. There must be hundreds.
Andrew	Where'd they come from?
Simon	Who knows? Let's pull them in.

(All tug at nets.)

Partner	The nets are going to break.

(Simon gestures to James and John to come. They get in their boat and row.)

Simon	Help us take these fish in. Put half in your boat.

(All take the nets into the boats.)

John	Hey, the boats are about to sink!

James	Isn't this fantastic?
Simon	*(falling on knees before Jesus)* Depart from me, Lord, for I am a sinful man.
Jesus	*(to Simon)* Do not be afraid. From now on you will be catching people.
Narrator	With that the fishermen brought their boats to land, left everything, and became followers of Jesus.

Walking on the Sea

Matthew 14:22-33   Mark 6:45-52   John 6:16-21

(Jesus, Peter, and Disciples face Crowd.)

Narrator   It is the end of a long day of teaching.

Jesus   *(to Disciples)*
You take the boat and go ahead to the other side of the lake. I'm going to say goodby to the people and pray awhile.

(Disciples board boat and begin rowing. Jesus waves Crowd off. Crowd exits. Jesus walks to the far side of stage and kneels.)

Narrator   Sometime between three and six o'clock in the morning the disciples were in the middle of the lake.

(Disciples have a hard time rowing.)

Disciple 1   We're hardly getting anywhere.

Disciple 2   Well, the wind is directly against us.

(Jesus walks toward them.)

Disciple 3   Say, what's that light?

Disciple 1   It looks like it's coming toward us.

Disciples
1,2,3   It's a ghost! *(They scream.)*

Jesus   Take courage. It is I. Don't be afraid.

Peter   Lord, if it's really you. tell me to come to you across the water.

Jesus   Come.

(Peter climbs out of boat and starts walking to Jesus.)

Peter   The wind! *(Starts to sink.)* Save me, Lord!

(Jesus grabs hold of his arm.)

Jesus   O you of little faith! Why did you doubt?

(Jesus and Peter walk to boat and climb in.)

Disciple 2   Hey, the wind died down.

(Disciples bow down before Jesus.)

Disciples
1,2,3
and Peter   Truly, you are the Son of God.

The Tax Money in the Fish

Matthew 17:24-27

Narrator Rome didn't tax its citizens because it received enough money from the foreign countries it conquered. Since the Jewish people were part of the Roman Empire, they had to pay taxes to Rome. In addition, each Jewish man paid a half-shekel tax every year for the upkeep of the temple. When Jesus and his disciples entered Capernaum, the temple tax collectors came to Peter.

(Peter walks alone. Tax Collectors 1, 2 come toward him. Jesus sits some distance away.)

Tax Collector 1 Doesn't your master pay the temple tax?

Peter Of course, he does. Wait a minute.

(Peter goes into the house where Jesus is.)

Narrator Before Peter can say a word about the tax, Jesus speaks to him.

Jesus What is your opinion, Simon? Do the kings of the world tax their citizens—or foreigners?

Peter Foreigners.

Jesus Then the citizens don't have to pay. But we don't want to offend these people. Go to the lake, drop in a line, and take in the first fish you hook. In its mouth you will find a coin worth enough for your temple tax and mine. Take it and give it to them for you and me.

Peter   If you say so.

(*Peter takes fishing pole and goes out.*)

Peter   (*to Tax Collectors*)
I'll be right back.

(*Peter catches fish and removes coin.*)

Peter   (*to himself*)
Now how did he know this was here?

(*Peter goes to Tax Collectors.*)

Peter   (*handing coin to Tax Collector 1*)
Here, this is the temple tax for Jesus and me.

Tax
Collector 1   Thank you.

Tax
Collector 2   Have a good day.

(*Tax Collectors exit.*)

The Second Large Catch of Fish

John 21:1-14

(Peter, Thomas, Nathanael, James, John, and Disciples are seated some distance from the boat.)

Narrator	After the resurrection some of the disciples were by the Sea of Tiberias.
Peter	*(standing up)* I'm going fishing.
Disciples	We'll go with you.

(Disciples go to boat and sit in it. Peter pushes the boat off and then jumps in. All begin to row.)

Narrator	The disciples fished all night, but when dawn came, they had caught nothing. Someone called to them from the shore.

(Jesus enters.)

Jesus	*(raising his hand to his mouth to shout)* Children, have you caught anything to eat?
Disciples	No.
Jesus	Cast the net over the right side of the boat and you will find something.

(Disciples cast their net to the right side of the boat.)

Thomas	Look at all the huge fish!
Nathanael	Every fish in the sea must be here.

(Disciples struggle to pull up net.)

James	We can't even haul the net up.
John	*(to Peter)* It is the Lord!

(Peter throws on cloak, jumps overboard, and swims to Jesus. The two talk for a while and then watch the others come in.)

Thomas	We'll never be able to lift this net on board. Let's just tow it behind us.

(Disciples row to shore, get out of boat, and join Jesus and Peter.)

Nathanael	Look, he has some bread, and fish is cooking over a charcoal

Jesus	Bring some of the fish you have just caught.
	(Peter goes to the boat and drags the net to shore.)
Peter	All these big fish and the net isn't breaking. *(to John)* Let's count them.
Jesus	Come, have breakfast. *(Disciples sit in a circle around Jesus. He takes the bread, and passes it out to them. Then he serves them the fish.)*
Narrator	When the disciples counted the fish, they found that there were one hundred and fifty-three. No one asked the man who he was. They knew it was the Lord.

A Possessed Man

Mark 1:21-28 Luke 4:31-37

(Jesus stands facing the Crowd and Persons 1, 2.)

Narrator — One sabbath Jesus was teaching in the synagogue in Capernaum when a man possessed by an evil spirit interrupted him.

Jesus — I say to you, God is a loving Father.

Person 1 — *(to Person 2)*
This Jesus is not like our other teachers.

Person 2 — No, he teaches with authority.

Jesus — And so, my brothers and sisters...

(Man enters, screaming.)

Man — Ai! What do you want with us, Jesus of Nazareth? Have you come to destroy us? I know who you are...the Holy One of God.

Jesus — Be quiet! Come out of him.

(Man shakes, falls to the ground, gives a loud scream, and then stops suddenly.)

Person 1 — *(to Man)*
Are you all right?

Man — Yes, I'm fine.

Person 2 — *(to Person 1)*
What does this mean?

Person 1 — Here is new teaching with authority.

Person 2 — He even commands evil spirits and they obey him.

Narrator — Jesus' reputation spread quickly all through Galilee.

Demons Sent Into Swine

Matthew 8:28-34   Mark 5:1-20   Luke 8:26-39

Narrator One day Jesus and his disciples sailed across the Lake of Galilee. They came to the land of the Gerasenes, who were not Jewish. Jesus had just set foot on the shore when a man possessed by demons came toward him. For a long time this man had lived in burial caves. He did not wear clothes, and day and night he howled and cut himself with stones. When people tried to chain him, he broke out of the chains.

(Swineherds stand at the side. Jesus and Disciples 1 and 2 enter. Man runs toward Jesus, gives a loud cry, and throws himself at his feet.)

Man *(shouting)*
Jesus, Son of the Most High God, what do you want with me?

Jesus Come out of the man, evil spirit!

Man I beg you. Don't punish me.

Jesus What is your name?

Man My name is Legion, for there are many of us. Please do not send us away from here and into the depths of the earth. Let us enter the pigs.

Jesus Go.

Narrator There was a herd of about two thousand pigs nearby. To the Jewish people, pigs were the most unclean animal. The demons went out of the man and into the pigs. The whole herd then rushed down the cliff into the lake and were drowned.

(Jesus, Disciples, and Man walk off to the side. The Man sits at Jesus' feet. Swineherds walk to front, and Persons 1, 2, 3 enter and stay at a distance.)

Swineherd 1 I don't believe it.

Swineherd 2 Come on. Let's go tell everyone in the field and the village.

(Swineherds run to Persons 1, 2, 3.)

Swineherd 1 The man from the tombs is cured.

Swineherd 2 A stranger sent the demons out of him.

Swineherd 1	They went into our pigs.
Swineherd 2	The pigs charged into the lake and were drowned.
	(Swineherds with Persons 1, 2, 3 return to Jesus.)
Person 1	Look at the man from the tombs. He's wearing clothes.
Person 3	And he's talking calmly. Wow!
Swineherd 1	*(pointing to Jesus)* He's the one who ordered the demons out of him.
Man	Yes, they went from me into the herd of pigs.
Swineherd 2	You should have seen those pigs squealing and stampeding into the water.
Person 2	*(to Person 1)* If this man has such power over demons, what will he do next? I'm scared.
Person 3	So am I.
Person 1	*(to Jesus)* Please leave.
Person 3	Yes, go to some other town.
Jesus	*(to Disciples)* Let's go. Get into the boat.
	(Jesus and Disciples begin to walk away. Man follows.)
Man	*(to Jesus)* Please, let me go with you.
Jesus	No, go home to your family and tell what God in his mercy has done for you.
	(Man returns to Persons 1, 2, 3. Jesus and Disciples exit.)
Man	*(to Person 1)* God did a great thing for me today. Let me tell you about it.

A Possessed, Blind, Mute Man

Matthew 12:22-28 Luke 11:14-20

(Jesus is with Persons 3, 4, Pharisees 1, 2, and the Crowd. Persons 1 and 2 lead the blind Possessed Man to him.)

Person 1 Jesus, this man is possessed by a devil.

Person 2 He can't see or talk.

(Possessed Man grunts. Jesus puts his hand on the man's shoulders.)

Jesus Be healed.

Possessed Man *(excitedly)*
I see. I see again. Oh, thank you, Master.

Person 3 *(to Person 4)*
Did you hear him? It's amazing.

Person 4 Incredible!

Person 3 Could this perhaps be the Son of David?

Pharisee 1 This man drives out demons only by the power of Beelzebul, the prince of demons.

Pharisee 2 Jesus, work a miracle to show that God approves of you.

Jesus Any country divided against itself will not last. A town or family divided against itself will fall apart. If Satan drives out Satan, he is divided against himself. How will his kingdom stand? You say that it is by Beelzebul that I drive out demons.

Pharisees 1, 2 Yes, yes.

Jesus Then how do your followers drive them out? But if it is by the Spirit of God that I drive out demons, then the kingdom of God has come upon you.

Peter's Mother-in-Law

Matthew 8:14-15   Mark 1:29-31   Luke 4:38-39

(Mother-in-Law is in bed. Peter, Peter's Wife, and Andrew are seated around her. Jesus, James, and John are some distance away.)

Narrator One day Jesus went with some of his disciples to the house of Peter and Andrew.

(Jesus, James, and John go to Peter's house.)

Jesus Peter, Andrew. Are you home?

(Peter comes to door.)

Peter Come in. Come in. We're worried about my mother-in-law.

Andrew She has such a high fever.

Peter's Wife She doesn't even recognize me—her own daughter. Won't you help her, Jesus?

Peter Yes, you can make her better if anyone can, Master.

(Jesus takes the Mother-in-Law's hand.)

Jesus *(to fever)*
Leave the body of this woman.

(Mother-in-Law sits up.)

Peter's Wife Mother, are you all right?

Mother-in-Law I feel wonderful. Very rested. What are you all staring at? *(Gets up.)* You men look hungry. Jesus, what can I fix for you to eat? I've got some nice fresh bread here.

Jesus Anything will be fine.

Peter Thank you, Jesus.

A Leper

Matthew 8:1-4   Mark 1:40-45   Luke 5:12-15

Narrator   As Jesus went through Galilee, a man covered with leprosy, a terrible skin disease, came to him. The man longed to be made clean so he could come back into contact with other people.

(Jesus walks along slowly. Leper hobbles up to him and kneels before him.)

Leper   Lord, if you wish, you can make me clean.

Jesus   *(stretching out his hand and touching him)*
Of course I want to. Be cured.

Leper   *(looking at hands)*
I'm cured. I'm clean. Oh, thank you, thank you!

Jesus   Listen, don't tell anyone about this. Go show yourself to the priest and let him examine you. Then offer for your cure the sacrifice that Moses ordered. This will prove to everyone that you are cured.

(Leper rises and walks toward Persons 1, 2. Jesus walks in the opposite direction.)

Leper   You won't believe what just happened to me. I was a leper, but a man named Jesus healed me. He touched me and said "Be cured" and I was.

Person 1   Where is he?

Person 2   I'd like to meet this man.

Leper   *(gestures toward Jesus)*
Back there.

(Persons 1, 2 run after Jesus.)

Narrator   So large crowds continued to follow Jesus.

The Paralytic

Matthew 9:1-8   Mark 2:1-12   Luke 5:17-26

(Jesus, Teachers, and Persons sit on the floor. Jesus is teaching quietly. At a distance the Paralyzed Man is on a mat with the Friends around him.)

Narrator   One day Jesus was teaching in a house in Capernaum. A paralyzed man was brought to the house. His friends hoped Jesus would cure him.

Friend 1   Look at all the people.

Friend 2   They're even packed together outside in front of the door.

Friend 3   We'll never get in to Jesus.

Friend 4   We've carried him this far *(nodding to Paralyzed Man)*. We can't give up now.

Friend 1   You're right. We must find a way. Think hard.

Friend 2   I've got it. Let's climb up on the roof and break through right above where Jesus is.

Friend 3   Ah, then we can lower our friend down to Jesus.

Friend 4   Everyone will move out of the way for him then. Good thinking.

(*While the Narrator speaks, the Paralyzed Man moves so that his mat is in front of Jesus. The Friends step back.*)

Narrator   So the men made a hole in the flat roof and carefully lowered the Paralyzed Man on his mat. Jesus was glad to see how much faith the men had.

Jesus   (*looking at the Paralyzed Man*)
Courage, child, your sins are forgiven.

Teacher 1   (*aside*)
How dare he talk like this? This is blasphemy.

Teacher 2   (*aside*)
Only God can forgive sins.

Jesus   (*to Teachers*)
Why do you think such things in your heart? Which is easier to say, "Your sins are forgiven," or to say, "Rise, pick up your mat and walk"? To show that I have authority on earth to forgive sins...(*to Paralyzed Man*) I say to you, rise, pick up your mat, and go home.

Paralyzed Man   (*picking up mat*)
Blessed be God. (*Exits.*)

Person 1   We have never seen anything like this.

Person 2   How kind and merciful God is!

The Man With a Withered Hand

Matthew 12:9-14   Mark 3:1-6   Luke 6:6-11

(Jesus stands before a seated Crowd that includes the Man with the withered hand and the Pharisees. He mimes teaching them.)

Narrator   One sabbath Jesus went to a synagogue and taught. A man with a withered hand was in the crowd.

Pharisee 1   *(to Pharisee 2)*
Watch him closely. If he heals on the sabbath, he is breaking the Law.

Pharisee 2   Right.

(Jesus points to Man with withered hand.)

Jesus   Come up here before us.

(Man goes to Jesus.)

Jesus   *(to Crowd)*
I ask you What does our Law allow us to do on the sabbath? To help or to harm? To save a man's life or destroy it? What if one of you had a sheep and it fell into a pit on the sabbath? Will he not take hold of it and get it out? A person is far more precious than a sheep. So, it is lawful to help someone on the sabbath.

(Jesus looks around at the Crowd with anger and sadness.)

Jesus   *(to the Man)*
Stretch out your hand.

(Man stretches out hand.)

Man   Why it's as good as the other one. Thank you, Master.

(Crowd oohs and ahs. Man flexes hand and shows it to them.)

(Pharisees 1, 2, 3 leave Crowd and meet at a distance.)

Pharisee 1   We have to kill that man Jesus.

Pharisee 2   Yes, but how?

Pharisee 3   I have an idea...

The Centurion's Servant

Matthew 8:5-13   Luke 7:1-10

(Jesus walks with Crowd and Jewish Elder.)

Narrator
One day when Jesus entered Capernaum, a Roman officer came to him.

The officer was a centurion, which meant that he commanded about a hundred soldiers. Since he was not Jewish, entering his house would make Jesus unclean by Jewish law.

(Centurion enters and goes to Jesus.)

Centurion
Sir, my servant boy, who is very dear to me, is sick. He is lying at home, paralyzed and in great pain.

Jewish Elder
(to Jesus)
He deserves to have you do this for him. He loves our people. In fact, he built the synagogue for us.

Jesus
(to Centurion)
I will come and cure him.

Centurion
Lord, do not trouble yourself. I am not worthy to have you enter under my roof. Only say the word and my servant will be healed. I am under authority myself, and I have soldiers under me. I say to one, "Go," and he goes; and to another, "Come," and he comes. If I order my servant, "Do this," he does it.

Jesus
(to Crowd)
I tell you, nowhere in Israel have I found such faith. Many will come from the east and the west and sit down with Abraham, Isaac and Jacob at the feast in the kingdom of heaven, but those who should be in the kingdom will be turned out into the dark where they will cry and grind their teeth. *(to Centurion)* Go home. You have believed, so let this be done for you.

Centurion
Thank you, sir.

(Jesus and Crowd exit. Centurion walks on. Messenger enters and runs toward him.)

Messenger
Sir, sir. He is cured. He's walking around and talking as if nothing has happened.

Centurion
Thank God!

The Canaanite Woman

Matthew 15:21-28   Mark 7:24-30

(In the far background the Daughter is running about wildly. Jesus and Disciples walk along.)

Narrator   One day Jesus was walking with his disciples near non-Jewish cities. A Canaanite woman, a Gentile, came to him.

(Woman comes toward Jesus and Disciples.)

Woman   *(crying out)*
Lord, Son of David!

(Jesus walks on.)

Woman   Have pity on me, sir. My daughter has a demon and is terribly sick.

(Jesus walks on.)

Woman   *(shouting)*
Have mercy, sir.

Disciple 1   *(to Jesus)*
Jesus, please give her what she wants and send her away.

Disciple 2   She's following us and making all this noise!

Jesus   *(turning to Woman)*
I was sent only to the lost sheep of the people of Israel.

(Woman catches up and falls at his feet.)

Woman   Lord, help me.

Jesus   It isn't right to take the children's food and throw it to the pups.

Woman   That's true, sir. But even pups eat the scraps that fall from the family's table.

Jesus   Woman, you have great faith! What you want will be done for you.

(Daughter lies calmly on bed.)

(Woman rises and walks toward Daughter. Jesus and Disciples exit.)

Woman   *(seeing Daughter)*
She's well.
(Raises her arms.) Thanks be to God!

A Deaf Mute

Mark 7:31

Narrator	As Jesus entered the district of the Ten Cities, some people brought him a deaf man with a serious speech defect.
	(Persons 1, 2, and 3 bring Deaf Mute to Jesus.)
Person 1	He can't hear at all.
Person 2	And he can hardly speak.
Person 3	Please lay your hands on him and cure him.
Jesus	*(to Deaf Mute)* Come with me. *(Jesus takes Deaf Mute away from Crowd. Deaf Mute's back is to the audience. Jesus mimes the actions while the Narrator describes them.)*
Narrator	Jesus puts his fingers into the man's ears. Then he spat and touched the man's tongue.
	(Jesus looks up to heaven and sighs.)
Jesus	Ephphatha. Be opened.
Deaf Mute	I heard you!
Person 1	Listen. He spoke plainly!
Deaf Mute	I can hear them, too.
Jesus	*(to all)* Do not tell anyone what happened here.
	(Jesus exits. Person 4 enters.)
	(Persons 1, 2, 3 and Deaf Mute run to meet Person 4.)
Person 1	Jesus cured this man who was deaf.
Person 2	He also made him speak clearly.
Person 3	He has done all things well! He makes the deaf hear and the mute speak.
Person 4	Let's go tell our friends and relatives.
	(All exit.)

An Epileptic Boy

Matthew 17:14-20   Mark 9:14-29   Luke 9:37-43

(Jesus and Disciples 1, 2, 3 join the Crowd which is talking excitedly to Disciple 4.)

Jesus   *(to Disciple 4)*
What are you arguing about with them?

Father   *(kneeling at Jesus' feet)*
Lord, have pity on my son— my only son. I brought him to you because he has an evil spirit and cannot talk. The spirit throws him to the ground and he foams at the mouth, grits his teeth, and becomes still. I asked your disciples to heal him, but they couldn't.

Jesus   Bring the boy to me.

(Father brings the Boy. Boy falls to the ground.)

Jesus   How long has this been happening to him?

Father   Ever since he was a child. He often falls into the fire and water. Have pity on us and help us if you can.

Jesus   If you can? Everything is possible to one who has faith.

Father   *(crying out)*
I do believe! Help my unbelief.

Jesus   *(to Boy)*
Deaf and dumb spirit, I command you, Come out of the boy and never enter him again!

(Boy screams and then lies still.)

Crowd *(to one another)*
He is dead.

(Jesus takes the Boy by the hand and helps him up. He puts the Boy's hand into the Father's hand. The Crowd gasps.)

Father Son. My son. You're going to be all right.

Person
in Crowd How great and mighty is our God!

(Crowd closes in around Father and Boy. Jesus and Disciples walk away.)

Disciple 1 Why couldn't we drive out this evil spirit?

Jesus It was because you do not have enough faith. If you had faith as big as a mustard seed, you could say to the hill, "Go from here to there," and it would move. You could do anything.

The Infirm Woman
Luke 13:10-17

(Jesus is standing and teaching the Crowd. Woman is in the Crowd. Chief of Synagogue and Opponents watch.)

Narrator One sabbath Jesus was teaching in the synagogue. A woman was there who for eighteen years had been possessed by a spirit that made her very weak. She was bent over and couldn't stand straight.

(Jesus notices the Woman.)

Jesus Come to me.

(Woman hobbles over to Jesus.)

Jesus Woman, you are free of your infirmity.

(Jesus lays his hands on her shoulders. Immediately she stands up straight.)

Woman Thanks be to God. He's cured me in his great mercy.

Chief *(to Crowd)*
There are six days for working. Come on those days to be cured, not on the sabbath day.

Jesus You hypocrites! Which of you does not untie his ox or his donkey and take him out of the stall on the sabbath to give it water? Satan has kept this daughter of Abraham here in bonds for eighteen years. Shouldn't she be set free on the sabbath?

(Chief and Opponents shake heads, shrug shoulders, and move back.)

Person 1 Isn't it marvelous what Jesus does?

Person 2 He brings happiness wherever he goes.

The Man With Dropsy

Luke 14:1-6

Narrator	One sabbath day Jesus went to eat at the house of one of the leading Pharisees. A man whose arms and legs were swollen with dropsy was also there.
	(Pharisees, Guests, and Man are gathered together. Jesus enters.)
Pharisee 1	Jesus, welcome. Please come in.
Jesus	Thank you.
	(Jesus stands opposite the Man.)
Pharisee 1	*(to Pharisee 2)* Watch him closely.
Pharisee 2	I intend to.
Jesus	*(to Pharisee 1 and 2)* Is it lawful to cure on the sabbath or not?
	(Silence)
Jesus	*(taking the Man by the shoulders)* Be healed.
Man	*(looking at his hands)* I'm cured. I'm cured. Thank you.
Jesus	Go on your way.
	(Man exits happily.)
Jesus	*(to Pharisees)* If one of you had a son or an ox that fell into a pit, wouldn't you pull him out immediately on the sabbath day?
	(Silence)
Narrator	The Pharisees were unable to answer.

The Ten Lepers
Luke 17:11-19

(Lepers stand at one side of room. Jesus at the other.)

Narrator Leprosy is a terrible disease that is easily spread. Lepers, people with leprosy, lived together outside of town. They were not allowed to come into contact with others. Lepers who thought they were cured went to the priests. If the priests declared that they were perfectly healed, then they could return home. One day Jesus was on his way to Jerusalem. *(Jesus walks toward Lepers.)* As he entered a village, ten lepers came to meet him.

Leper 1 There he is. I see him. Come on.

(Lepers go forward a little and call from a distance.)

Lepers 2, 3 Jesus!

Lepers 4, 5 Master!

Lepers 6, 7, 8, 9 Have pity on us!

Jesus Go to the priests and let them examine you.

Lepers Yes, Master.

(Lepers turn back. Jesus walks on.)

Leper 6 Say, my back doesn't hurt any more.

Leper 7 And my legs are straight again. *(Tosses cane aside.)*

Leper 8 Look at my hands. The skin is like new.

Leper 9 *(to Samaritan Leper)*
Your face is as fresh and clear as a young man's.

Ten Lepers We're healed! We're healed!

Samaritan Leper *(Lepers move on quickly.)*
Jesus cured us. *(Turns away from group and walks back toward Jesus.)*

Praise God! Blessed be the Lord who healed me. God is my strength and my salvation. *(Falls at Jesus' feet.)* Thank you, Jesus, for making me whole again.

Jesus   You're welcome. But weren't ten men healed? Where are the other nine? Only the foreigner has come back to thank God. Stand up and go. *(Helps the man up.)* Your faith has saved you.

(Samaritan Leper follows the other Lepers.)

Narrator   The man who came back to thank God was a Samaritan, not a Jewish person. Jesus invites all people into the kingdom of his Father.

Blind Bartimaeus

Matthew 20:29-34   Mark 10:46-52   Luke 18:35-43

(Bartimaeus is seated. Bystanders 1, 2, 3 are around him.)

Narrator
: As Jesus and his disciples left Jericho, a large crowd followed them. Bartimaeus, a blind beggar, was sitting at the side of the road.

(Jesus and Crowd enter and walk toward Bartimaeus and Bystanders 1, 2, 3.)

Bartimaeus
: *(to Bystanders)*
  I hear a great crowd coming. What's going on?

Bystander 1
: Jesus of Nazareth is leaving the town. He's coming down this road.

Bartimaeus
: *(shouting)*
  Jesus! Son of David! Have pity on me!

Bystander 1
: Be quiet.

Bystander 2
: Don't make such a scene!

Bystander 3
: You're embarrassing us.

Bartimaeus
: *(more loudly)*
  Son of David, have pity on me.

Jesus
: *(to Bystanders)*
  Call him here.

Bystander 1
: *(to Bartimaeus)*
  Don't be afraid.

Bystander 2
: Get up. He is calling you.

(Bartimaeus throws off cloak, jumps up, and walks blindly toward Jesus.)

Jesus
: What do you want me to do for you?

Bartimaeus
: Master, I want to see.

Jesus
: Go your way. Your faith has saved you.

Bartimaeus
: *(excitedly)*
  I can see you! I can see! Praise God!

(The Crowd cheers.)

(Jesus, Crowd, and Bartimaeus move on together.)

The Nobleman's Son

John 4:46-54

Narrator	When Jesus was in Cana, a royal official in Capernaum had a son who was sick. On hearing that Jesus was nearby, the man went to him for help.
	(Nobleman walks up to Jesus.)
Nobleman	Please, Jesus, I beg you come down to Capernaum and cure my son. He is near death.
Jesus	Unless you people see signs and wonders, you will not believe.
Nobleman	Sir, come down before my child dies.
Jesus	Return home. Your son will live.
	(Nobleman walks away. Jesus exits.)
Narrator	The next day as the nobleman was on his way home, his servants met him.
	(Servants enter.)
Servant 1	Master, master!
Servant 2	Your boy is going to live.
Nobleman	What time did he begin to recover?
Servant 1	The fever left him yesterday about one in the afternoon.
Nobleman	That's the very hour Jesus told me he would live.
	(The Nobleman and Servants exit excitedly.)
Narrator	The nobleman and his whole household became believers.

Cure at the Pool at Bethesda

John 5:1-18

(Man and Sick People are on mats. Crowd is nearby.)

Narrator　One day Jesus went up to Jerusalem for a Jewish feast. By the Sheep Gate was a pool called Bethesda. It had five porches crowded with the blind, the lame, and the paralyzed. They were waiting there for the movement of the water, for after the water moved, the first person to go into it was cured. One man lying there had been sick for thirty-eight years. Jesus knew this.

(Jesus enters and goes to Man.)

Jesus　Do you want to be well?

Man　Sir, I have no one to put me into the pool when the water is stirred up. While I am on my way, someone else gets down there before me.

Jesus　Rise, take up your mat, and walk.

(Man stands, picks up mat, and walks. Jesus disappears into Crowd. Pharisees 1, 2 enter and stop the Man.)

Pharisee 1　It is the sabbath.

Pharisee 2　You are not allowed to carry that mat on the sabbath.

Man　But the man who made me well told me, "Take up your mat and walk."

Pharisee 1　Who is this person who told you to take it up and walk?

Man　I have no idea, and I don't see him now in this crowd.

(Man moves on and stands alone. Pharisees stand some distance away.)

Narrator　Later, Jesus found the man in the temple area.

(Jesus goes to Man.)

Jesus　Look, you are well. Do not sin any more so that nothing worse may happen to you.

Man　Yes, sir. Thank you, sir. What is your name?

Jesus　I am Jesus. *(Exits.)*

(Man goes to Pharisees.)

Man　The one who made me well is Jesus.

Pharisee 2　Jesus again. We might have known.

The Man Born Blind
John 9:1-41

(Blind Man is seated on the ground. Jesus and Disciples enter.)

Narrator One sabbath as Jesus walked along with his disciples, he saw a man who had been blind from birth.

Disciple 1 Rabbi, was it his sin or the sin of his parents that caused him to be born blind?

Jesus Neither. He is blind so that God's works might show forth in him. We have to do the work of the one who sent me while it is day. Night is coming when no one can work. While I am in the world, I am the light of the world.

(Jesus helps Man stand. Then he mimes the action as the Narrator describes them.)

Narrator Jesus spat on the ground, made some mud, and rubbed the man's eyes with it.

Jesus *(to Man)*
Go wash in the pool at Siloam.

(Man goes to side and splashes water on his face.)

Man I can see! I can see!

(Jesus and Disciples exit. Man walks along. Neighbors enter.)

Neighbor 1 Isn't this the one who used to sit and beg?

Neighbor 2 It sure is.

Neighbor 3 No, he just looks like him.

Man I am the man.

Neighbor 1 Then how were your eyes opened?

Man The man called Jesus made mud and rubbed it on my eyes. Then he told me, "Go to Siloam and wash." So I went there and washed and was able to see.

Neighbor 2 Where is he?

Man I don't know.

(Pharisees and Messenger enter. Neighbors take Man to them.)

Neighbor 2 This man was blind, but Jesus made him see.

Pharisee 1	How did he do it?
Man	He put mud on my eyes, I washed it off, and now I can see.
Pharisee 2	That man cannot be from God because he does not obey the sabbath law.
Pharisee 3	But if a man is a sinner, how can he perform miracles like these?
Pharisee 2	Since it was your eyes he opened, what do *you* have to say about him?
Man	He is a prophet.
Pharisee 2	*(to Pharisee 1)* He probably wasn't blind from birth.
Pharisee 1	You're right. Let's question his parents.
Pharisee 2	*(to Messenger)* Tell the man's parents to come here.

(Messenger leaves and returns with Mother and Father while Pharisees motion as if arguing.)

Pharisee 1	Is this your son?
Pharisee 2	Was he really blind from birth?
Pharisee 3	And if so, how does he see now?
Father	We know that this is our son.
Mother	And that he was born blind.
Father	We do not know how he sees now, nor do we know who opened his eyes.
Mother	Ask him. He is old enough to speak for himself.

(Father, Mother, and Man exit.)

Narrator	The parents were afraid of the Pharisees. Anyone who accepted Jesus as the Messiah was put out of the synagogue.
Pharisee 1	*(to Messenger)* Bring the man here.

(Messenger exits and returns with the Man.)

Pharisee 2	Give glory to God by telling the truth. First of all, we know this man is a sinner.
Man	I do not know if he is a sinner or not. One thing I do know is that I was blind and now I can see.

Pharisee 3	What did he do to you? How did he open your eyes?
Man	I told you already and you would not listen. Why do you want to hear it again? Do you want to become his disciples, too?
Pharisee 1	You are that man's disciple. We are disciples of Moses! We know that God spoke to Moses, but we do not know where this man is from.
Man	Well, here is a strange thing. You do not know where he is from, yet he opened my eyes. We know that God does not listen to sinners, but that if someone is devout and does his will, he listens to him. It is unheard of that anyone ever gave sight to a person born blind. If the man were not from God, he could never have done such a thing.
Pharisees 1, 2, 3	What!
Pharisee 1	You were born totally in sin and are you trying to teach us?
	(Pharisees grab the Man and throw him out. Man walks away. Pharisees talk in circle. Neighbors go to Jesus.)
Neighbor 1	*(to Jesus)* The Pharisees threw the man you healed out of the synagogue.
	(Neighbor exits. Jesus looks for Man and catches up to him.)
Jesus	Do you believe in the Son of Man?
Man	Who is he, sir, that I may believe in him?
Jesus	You have seen him and the one speaking with you is he.
Man	*(bowing low)* I do believe, Lord.
	(Pharisees 2, 3 walk by.)
Jesus	I came into this world for judgment, to make the sightless see and the seeing blind.
Pharisee 3	You are not calling us blind, are you?
Jesus	If you were blind you would have no sin, but since you say, "We see," your sin remains.
	(The Pharisees exit in one direction; Jesus and the Man in another.)

Raising the Widow's Son

Luke 7:11-17

Narrator   Jesus was on his way south to the village of Nain. A great number of disciples and other people were with him. Near the gate of the town they met a large funeral procession going out from the city.

(Jesus and Followers walk toward funeral procession. Man is on bier. If he is not carried, the Mourners move forward only slightly and Bearers only pretend to walk. Widow walks in front, crying and supported by Woman.)

Follower 1   *(to Mourner 1)*
Who are you burying?

Mourner 1   A young man from our town.

Mourner 2   His mother is a widow. He was all she had.

Jesus   *(to Widow)*
Don't cry.

(Jesus goes to the bier and puts his hand on it. The Bearers stop.)

Jesus   *(to Man)*
Young man, I tell you, arise.

(Man sits up. Crowd gasps and steps back in awe.)

Man   *(rubbing eyes)*
Where am I? What's going on?

(Jesus helps Man off bier.)

Jesus   *(to Widow)*
Here is your son back.

Widow   My son! Thanks be to God.

Mourner 1   A great prophet has appeared among us.

Follower 2   God has visited his people.

Raising Jairus's Daughter and Healing the Sick Woman

Matthew 9:18-26   Mark 5:21-43   Luke 8:40-56

(Jesus is seated teaching Crowd. Peter, James, John, and Persons 1, 2 are there. Jairus enters and throws himself down at Jesus' feet.)

Jairus   Please, sir, come to my house. My little girl, who is only twelve, is dying. Lay your hand on her so that she may get well.

Person 1   Who is that man?

Person 2   Jairus, the official of the synagogue.

(Jesus stands and moves with Jairus and Disciples. People crowd them. Woman enters, goes through Crowd, and comes behind Jesus.)

Woman   If I can just touch his clothes, I shall be cured.

(Woman touches the edge of Jesus' cloak. Jesus stops.)

Jesus   Who touched me?

Person 1   Not me.

Person 2   I didn't touch you.

Peter   Master, all these people are pushing and pressing in upon you, and you ask who touched you?

Jesus   Someone has touched me, for I know that power has gone out from me.

(Jesus looks around. Woman, trembling, kneels at his feet.)

Woman   I did it. For twelve years I've been suffering from bleeding. No doctor has been able to help me. Although I spent all my money, I only got worse. The instant I touched your cloak, I was healed.

Jesus   Courage, my daughter; your faith has saved you. Go in peace and be free of this illness.

Woman   *(rising)*
Thank you, Master.

(Messenger enters and goes to Jairus.)

Messenger   Jairus, your daughter has died. Why bother the teacher any longer?

Jesus	*(to Jairus)* Don't be afraid. Just have faith and she will be saved. Peter, James, and John, come with us. The rest of you stay here.
	(Crowd exits. Mourners enter, crying and wailing. Jesus, Jairus, Peter, James, and John go to them. Mother enters. Girl enters and lies on mat.)
Jesus	*(to Mourners)* What's all this noise? Stop crying. The child is not dead but asleep.
Mourner 1	*(mocking)* Sure she's sleeping. Everyone stops breathing when they're sleeping.
Mourner 2	*(laughing)* Hope you don't plan to stay around until she wakes up.
Mourner 3	You must be crazy.
Jesus	*(to Mourners)* Leave this house right now. All of you. *(to Mother, Jairus, Peter, James, and John)* Come.
	(Jesus takes Girl by the hand.)
Jesus	Little girl, I say to you arise.
	(Girl gets up and walks around.)
Girl	Hello. I must have fallen asleep. Mom, Dad, who are these people?
Jairus	Friends, dear.
Mother	*(to Jairus)* What power he has. *(Goes to Girl and hugs her.)*
Jesus	Do not tell anyone what happened here. Now give her something to eat.

The Raising of Lazarus
John 11:1-44

(Jesus is seated with Disciples. Martha, Mary, and Mourners are seated in a far corner. Lazarus is behind large box some distance away. Messenger runs to Jesus.)

Messenger   Jesus, I have a message for you from Martha and Mary at Bethany. They say, "Lord, your dear friend Lazarus is sick."

Jesus   This sickness will not end in death. This has happened in order to bring glory to God and to the Son of God.

Narrator   Although Jesus loved his three friends in Bethany, he stayed where he was for two more days. Then he decided to go to them.

Jesus   Let us go back to Judea.

Disciple 1   Teacher, a little while ago the people there wanted to stone you. And you want to go back?

Jesus   Our friend Lazarus has fallen asleep, but I am going to wake him.

Disciple 2   Master, if he is asleep, the worst is over.

Disciple 3   He will get well.

Jesus   Lazarus is dead, but for your sake I am glad that I was not there so that you may believe. Let's go to him.

Thomas   *(to other Disciples)*
Let us also go to die with him!

(Group walks toward Mourners.)

Narrator   When Jesus and disciples arrived in Bethany, they find out that Lazarus has already been in the tomb for four days. Friends and relatives were still at the house of Mary and Martha comforting them. When Martha heard that Jesus was coming, she left the house to meet him.

(Martha gets up and walks to meet Jesus.)

Martha   *(to Jesus)*
Lord, if you had been here, my brother would not have died. But even now I know that whatever you ask of God, God will give you.

Jesus   Your brother will rise.

Martha   I know that he will rise in the resurrection on the last day.

Jesus	I am the resurrection and the life. Whoever believes in me even if he dies will live, and everyone who lives and believes in me will never die. Do you believe this?
Martha	Yes, Lord, I have come to believe that you are the Messiah, the Son of God, who is coming into the world.
Jesus	Where's Mary?
Martha	She's at home. I'll get her.
	(Martha runs back to the house. Jesus stays where he is.)
Martha	Mary. Mary, can I see you alone a minute?
	(Mourners draw back.)
Mary	What is it?
Martha	The teacher is here, asking for you.
	(Mary gets up and goes quickly to Jesus.)
Mourner 1	She must be going to the tomb to weep there.
Mourner 2	Let's go with her.

(*Mourners follow Mary. Mary throws herself at Jesus' feet. She and Mourners are crying.*)

Mary	Lord, if you had been here, my brother would not have died!
Jesus	(*sighing*) Where have you laid him?
Mourner 1	Sir, come and see.

(*Group moves toward Lazarus. Jesus wipes his eyes.*)

Mourner 2	See how much he loved him!
Mourner 3	He gave sight to the blind man. Couldn't he have kept Lazarus from dying?

(*Group stops a way from Lazarus. Jesus goes toward tomb.*)

Jesus	Take away the stone.
Martha	Lord, by now there will be a bad smell. He has been dead for four days.
Jesus	Didn't I tell you that if you believed you would see God's glory?

(*Men push stone away. Jesus looks up to heaven.*)

Jesus	Father, I thank you for hearing me. I know that you always hear me, but because of the crowd here I have said this that they may believe that you sent me. (*Loudly*) Lazarus, come out!

(*Lazarus comes forth. Crowd gasps.*)

Jesus	Untie him and let him go free.

(*Men unwrap Lazarus. Mary, Martha, and Jesus go up to him and hug him.*)

Mary and Martha	Lazarus! Lazarus!

The Lost Sheep
Matthew 18:12-14   Luke 15:3-7

(Shepherd is with Sheep. Lost Sheep is alone in corner on the floor.)

Jesus   Suppose a man has a hundred sheep.

Shepherd   *(counting sheep)*
96, 97, 98, 99. Uh, oh. One's missing. I bet he wandered off and got lost. I'll have to go after him. These others will be safe enough as they graze in the pasture.

(Searches for Lost Sheep.)

Lost Sheep   Baaaa.

Shepherd   I hear him. *(Spots Lost Sheep.)* Oh, there he is, too scared to move. I'11 have to pick him up and carry him home.

(to Lost Sheep) I'm so happy I found you. Don't be afraid now. You'll be all right.

(Shepherd and Lost Sheep exit.)

(Friends enter.)

Jesus   When the shepherd has his lost sheep back with the flock again, he calls his friends.

Shepherd   Joe, Matt, Judith, Ann, everybody! Come on over. Celebrate with me because I have found my lost sheep.

(Friends joyfully surround Shepherd, shake his hand, slap him on the back.)

Jesus   In the same way, there will be more joy in heaven over one sinner who repents than over ninety-nine people who do not need to repent.

The Lost Coin

Luke 15:8-10

(Woman is in the center. Sarah is on one side of her in the next house. She is stirring something. Rachel is beyond her in the next house. She is sleeping in a chair. On the other side of the woman Mary and James are seated and talking quietly to each other. Jesus speaks from the side of the stage.)

Jesus Once there was a poor woman who had ten silver coins...

Woman *(counting coins)*
One, two, three, four, five, six, seven, eight, nine. Nine? Let me count again. Two, four, six, eight, nine. Oh, no! One is missing. Where could it be? *(Looks around room.)* Maybe some light will help. *("Lights" candle and searches room.)* I know. I'll sweep the house. I might hear it clink against the hard, dirt floor. *(Sweeps.)* No luck.

I'll just have to search every inch of this house. *(Begins a careful search and spots the coin against a table leg.)* Aha! Here it is. Thank goodness.

(Goes to Sarah's house.)
Sarah, I've been looking everywhere for one of my coins. I just found it. Come on over and celebrate with me.

Sarah Sure. I'm always glad to celebrate.

Woman Would you run over to my cousin Rachel and invite her too? Thanks.

(Sarah goes to Rachel. The Woman goes to Mary and James, knocks, and calls out.)

Mary? James? Can you come to my house a while? I just found a coin I had lost. I'm so happy I have to celebrate. Bring all your children, too.

James Great. We'll be right over.

(All gather at woman's house.)

Jesus I tell you, the angels in heaven rejoice the same way over one sinner who repents.

The Prodigal Son

Luke 15:11-32

(Jesus is off to the side. Father is seated. Neighbor stands near. Employer is seated at a distance.)

Jesus   A man had two sons.

(Younger Son enters and goes to Father.)

Younger Son   Father, let me have my share of the estate that is coming to me.

Father   *(sadly)*
If that's what you really want. Call your brother here.

(Younger Son leaves. Father writes on two scrolls. Younger Son returns with Older Son.)

Father   *(to Older Son)*
Your brother wants his share of the inheritance now, so you might as well have yours, too. I have divided the property between you. Here. *(Gives each a scroll.)*

Sons   Thank you, Father.

(Father and Older Son exit. Younger Son goes to Neighbor.)

Younger Son   How would you like to buy half of our property? It belongs to me now, and I'm selling it.

Neighbor   How much are you asking for it?

Younger Son   Eighty thousand silver coins.

Neighbor   I'll give you fifty.

Younger Son   Seventy-five.

Neighbor   All right. Seventy-five. *(Leaves and returns with money bag. Hands it to him. Younger Son hands over scroll.)*

Younger Son   Thank you!

(Both exit.)

Jesus   The younger son went to a distant land. There he wasted all his money on drinking, gambling, and women. When a famine came to that country, the boy had nothing left to buy food.

(The Younger Son walks alone. He shakes the empty money bag upside-down and tosses it away.)

Younger Son   Guess I don't need that anymore. I'll have to get a job.

	(Goes to Employer.)
Younger Son	Pardon me, sir. Can you use some help on your property?
Employer	As a matter of fact, I can. I need someone to take care of the pigs on my farm.
Younger Son	I can do that.
Employer	Fine, you can start now. They're down the road. *(Points and exits.)*
	(Younger Son walks to farm, takes sack, and feeds pigs.)
Younger Son	I'm so hungry I could eat this pig food. No one said anything about my supper. My father's servants have more food than they can eat, and here I am starving. I will leave and return to my father and say, "Father, I have sinned against God and against you. I no longer deserve to be called your son. Treat me as one of your hired workers."
	(Son drops sack and walks toward home. Father enters with Servants 1, 2 and, shading his eyes, peers down road.)
Father	That looks like my boy. *(Runs to Younger Son and embraces him.)*
Younger Son	Father, I have sinned against God and against you. I no longer deserve to be called your son.
Father	*(Gestures for Servants to come)* Quick. Bring out the finest robe and put it on him. Put a ring on his finger and shoes on his feet. Then go kill the fattened calf. Let us celebrate with a feast. This son of mine was dead and has come back to life. He was lost and has been found.
	(Servants exit. Father and Younger Son walk to house. Servants 1, 2 bring robe, ring, and shoes and put them on the Younger Son. All exit except Servant 1. Music plays. Older Son enters.)
Older Son	*(to Servant 1)* Come here. Tell me, what's the reason for the music and dancing?
Servant 1	Your brother is home. Your father has killed the fattened calf because he has his son back safe and sound.
Older Son	*(folding arms and sitting)* Well, don't think I'm going to celebrate that.
	(Servant 1 exits. Shortly, the Father enters and goes to Older Son.)
Father	Son, please come in and join in the celebration.

Older Son Look, all these years I have served you. I never disobeyed your orders once. Yet you never gave me a young goat to feast on with my friends. But when this son of yours returns after wasting all your money— he and his women— you kill the fattened calf for him.

Father My son, you are with me always; everything I have is yours. But now we must celebrate and be happy. Your brother was dead and has come back to life. He was lost and has been found. Come on in.

(Older Son rises and both exit.)

The Weeds

Matthew 13:24-30

Jesus	The kingdom of heaven is like this. A man sowed good seed in his field.

(Sower enters casting "seeds" from basket. Servants 1, 2 enter. All stretch, yawn, and sleep.)

Jesus	One night while everyone was asleep, an enemy came and sowed seeds among the wheat. Then he made off.

(Enemy enters casting seeds from basket where the Sower did. Exits.)

Jesus	When the wheat grew and ripened, the weeds appeared, too. The servants noticed there was a problem.
Servant 1	*(to Sower)* Sir, didn't you sow good seed in your field? Where are all the weeds coming from?
Sower	An enemy has done this.
Servant 2	Do you want us to go and pull up the weeds?
Sower	No, because if you pull up the weeds, you might uproot the wheat along with them.
Servants 1,2	You're right.
Sower	Let the wheat and weeds grow together until harvest. Then at harvest time I will say to the workers, "First collect the weeds and tie them in bundles for burning. Then gather the wheat and put it in my barn."
Servants 1,2	Good idea, Master.

The Hidden Treasure

Matthew 13:44

(Jesus is at one side. Buyers 1, 2, 3 and Owner stand off to the side.)

Jesus   The kingdom of heaven is like this.

(Man walks along and stumbles.)

Man   *(stooping)* What's this? Hmmm. It looks like the corner of a chest. *(Digs up chest and opens it.)* Wow, it's a treasure chest full of coins and jewelry! *(Puts it back and covers it with dirt.)* I must buy this field. First I'll have to get some money.

(Man walks over to Buyers 1, 2, 3.)

Man   *(loudly)* House for sale. House for sale.

Buyer 1   I'm looking for a house. How much does yours cost?

Man   Five thousand silver coins.

Buyer 1   That's reasonable. What about the furniture? I need furniture, too.

Man   For two thousand more silver coins, you can have everything in the house.

Buyer 1	This must be my lucky day. Here's your money. *(Gives coins to Man and exits.)*
Man	*(loudly)* Donkey and sheep for sale.
Buyer 2	I'd like a donkey. How old is yours?
Man	Only two years old and he's healthy. You can have him for one thousand silver coins.
Buyer 2	It's a deal. *(Hands over coins and exits.)*
Buyer 3	How many sheep do you have?
Man	Five beautiful sheep.
Buyer 3	I'll give you one thousand silver coins for them.
Man	Three thousand.
Buyer 3	Two thousand.
Man	They're yours.
	(Buyer 3 hands coins to Man and exits.)
Man	Now I have enough money to buy that field. *(Goes to Owner.)* I'd like to buy your north field.
Owner	It's not for sale.
Man	I'll give you ten thousand silver coins for it.
Owner	Are you crazy? It's only worth half that much.
Man	Not to me.
Owner	OK. You can have it.
	(Man gives Owner the coins.)
Owner	Thank you! *(Exits.)*
Man	Thank *you*. *(Goes to field, digs up treasure, and hugs it.)* Ah, you're mine. All mine.

The Pearl of Great Price

Matthew 13:45-46

(Jesus is off to the side. Salesman is at desk.)

Jesus   The kingdom of heaven is like this.

(Man enters and approaches Salesman.)

Salesman   Hello. Can I help you?

Man   Yes. I've been looking everywhere for a beautiful pearl.

Salesman   We have an excellent collection of pearls. *(Takes out pearls.)* See what you think of these.

Man   *(after looking for a short time)*
These are nice, but I'm looking for something special.

Salesman   We do have one rare pearl. It's very expensive.

Man   Let me see it.

Salesman   *(taking out large pearl)*
Here it is. Isn't it lovely?

Man   *(Whistles in admiration)*
I have never seen such a pearl. It is so large and perfect. How much is it?

Salesman   Actually it's priceless, but we're selling it for twenty thousand silver coins.

Man   I can give you ten thousand for it.

Salesman   Eighteen and no lower.

Man   Twelve thousand.

Salesman   Fifteen thousand and that's final.

Man   I'll buy it. Would you hold it for me until I return tomorrow?

Salesman   I'd be glad to.

Jesus   The man went home and had a large sale. He sold his house, his livestock, and everything he owned. Finally, he had enough money to buy the pearl.

(Man returns to store.)

Man   *(to Salesman)*
        Hello. I came for my pearl. *(Puts down money.)*

Salesman   *(Counts money, then hands over pearl.)*
        Congratulations!

Man   Thank you. This is the happiest day of my life.

The Great Banquet

Luke 14:16-24

(Jesus is at far side. Master and Servant are at one side of stage, and Guests 1, 2, 3 are on opposite side.)

Jesus   There was once a man who planned a great banquet. He invited many people.

Master   *(to Servant)*
It's time for the feast. Go to my guests. Say to them, "Come, everything is ready!"

(Servant goes to Guest 1.)

Servant   It's time for my master's feast. Come. Everything is ready.

Guest 1   I have bought some land and must go and look at it. I'm sorry.

(Servant goes to Guest 2.)

Servant   It's time for my master's feast. Come. Everything is ready.

Guest 2   I have bought five pairs of oxen and am on my way to try them out. Please excuse me.

(Servant goes to Guest 3.)

Servant	It's time for my master's feast. Come. Everything is ready.
Guest 3	I've just gotten married, so I cannot come.
	(Servant returns to Master. Guests 1, 2, 3 exit. Poor Couple, Crippled Woman, Blind Man enter.)
Servant	Sir, none of your guests can come. They are all too busy.
Master	*(angrily)* What! After all the trouble I went to, they can't come! Hurry out to the streets and alleys of the town and bring back the poor, the crippled, the blind and the lame.
	(Servant goes to the Poor Couple, the Crippled Woman, and Blind Man.)
Servant	*(to Poor Couple)* My master is giving a grand feast. Come. *(to Blind Man)* Come to my master's feast. *(to Crippled Woman)* You're invited to my master's house for supper.
	(All go to Master.)
Servant	*(to Master)* Your order has been carried out, sir, but there is still room for more.
Master	Go out to the country roads then and make people come so that my house will be full. I tell you that none of those who were invited will taste my dinner.
Servant	Yes, sir.

The Wicked Vinedressers

Matthew 21:33-41   Mark 12:1-12   Luke 20:9-16

(Jesus is off to the side. Tenants 1, 2 are on one side. Landowner is on the other side. Servants 1, 2, 3 are near him.)

Jesus Listen to another parable. A man planted a vineyard on his land. He put a fence around it, dug a winepress, and built a tower. Then he leased it to tenants. They were to care for it while he was out of town. At harvest time he expected the tenants to give him his grapes.

(Landowner gestures for Servant 1 to come.)

Landowner *(to Servant 1)*
It's harvest time. Go to the tenants and collect my grapes from them.

(Servant goes to Tenants 1, 2.)

Servant *(to Tenants 1, 2)*
My master sent me for his grapes.

Tenant 1 Is that so? Well, he can't have them.

(Tenants beat Servant 1, who returns to the Landowner.)

Landowner What happened?

Servant 1 The tenants attacked me when I asked for the grapes.

Landowner Take care of your wounds.

(Servant 1 exits. Landowner gestures for Servant 2 to come.)

Landowner Go to the tenants on my land and ask for the harvest.

Servant 2 Yes, Master.
(Goes to Tenants.)
I've come for my master's grapes.

Tenant 2 Too bad.

(Tenants beat Servant 2, who returns to the Landowner.)

Landowner I see you had no luck.

Servant 2 They will not give you your grapes.

Landowner Take care of your wounds.

(Servant 2 exits. Landowner gestures for Servant 3 to come.)

Landowner Tell the tenants to hand over my grapes.

Servant 3	Yes, sir. *(Goes to Tenants.)* My master demands his grapes.
Tenant 1	Well, we're not going to give them to him. *(Tenants beat Servant 3, who returns to the Landowner.)*
Servant 3	Master, it's no use. They will not give you your grapes.
Landowner	Go, take care of your wounds. *(Servant 3 exits. Servant 4 enters.)*
Landowner	Maybe they will respect the son I love. *(to Servant 4)* Tell my son to come here. *(Servant 4 exits and returns with Son.)*
Landowner	Son, please go to the tenants and collect the grapes that belong to us.
Son	Yes, Father. *(Son walks toward Tenants.)*
Tenant 1	*(to Tenant 2)* Say, this is the heir coming.
Tenant 2	Come on, let's kill him and take over his inheritance. *(Tenants grab the Son, take him off to the side and "kill" him. Servants 1, 2, 3 enter and stand by Landowner. Then Servant 4 runs in.)*
Servant 4	*(to Landowner)* Sir, I bring you bad news. Your son's body has been found outside the vineyard. He's been killed.
Landowner	My son, my son! *(to Servants)* Come with me. We'll put an end to this. *(Servants 1, 2, 3, 4 and Landowner go to Tenants. Servants grab Tenants from behind.)*
Landowner	Greedy murderers! *(to Servants)* Take these men away and see that they get what they deserve. I'll find tenants who will give me grapes at the right times.
Jesus	The kingdom of heaven will be given to people who produce fruit.

The Workers in the Vineyard

Matthew 20:1-16

(Jesus is to the side. Workers stand in pairs.)

Jesus   The kingdom of heaven is like this. Once there was a man who went out early in the morning to hire workers for his vineyard.

(Employer enters and goes to First Workers.)

Employer   I need help in my vineyard. I'll pay you the usual day's wage, a silver coin. How about it?

First Workers   Great.

Employer   You know where my place is. Go to my vineyard and my foreman will tell you what to do.

(First Workers exit. Employer exits in the opposite direction.)

Jesus   At nine o'clock the employer again went to the marketplace.

(Employer enters and goes to Second Workers.)

Employer   You look like you're not doing anything. Go and work in my vineyard, and I'll pay you a fair wage.

Second Workers   O.K.

(Second Workers exit. Employer exits in the opposite direction.)

Jesus   At twelve o'clock the employer returned to the marketplace.

(Employer enters and goes to Third Workers.)

Employer   Would you like a job in my vineyard? Go now and I'll pay you tonight.

Third Workers   Sure.

(Third Workers exit. Employer exits in the opposite direction.)

Jesus   At three o'clock the employer again hired workers.

(Employer enters and goes to Fourth Workers.)

Employer   I'm hiring workers for my vineyard. Would you like a job?

Fourth Workers   Yes.

(Fourth Workers exit. Employer exits in the opposite direction.)

Jesus   It was almost five o'clock in the evening when the employer came again in the marketplace.

	(Employer enters and goes to Last Workers.)
Employer	Why are you wasting the whole day here doing nothing?
Last Workers	No one hired us.
Employer	Well, then, go work in my vineyard.
	(All exit.)
Jesus	At six o'clock in the evening the owner of the vineyard spoke to his foreman. *(Employer and Foreman enter.)*
Employer	Call the workers and give them their pay, but start with the last arrivals and end with the first.
Foreman	*(shouting)* The day's over. Come for your pay. Those who came last stand in line first.
	(Workers enter and set down baskets. They go to Foreman and stand two by two from Last Workers to First Workers hired. Employer stands nearby.)
Foreman	*(giving Last Workers each a coin)* Here's your silver coin.
First Worker 1	*(to First Worker 2)* Wow! Imagine what we'll get.
Foreman	*(giving each of the others a silver coin)* And here's yours...and yours... and yours...and yours...and yours...and yours...and yours...and yours.
First Worker 2	*(to First Worker 1)* That's not fair. We've been gypped.
First Worker 1	*(to Employer)* These workers who were hired last worked only one hour, while we did a hard day's work in the hot sun. Yet you paid them the same as you paid us!
Employer	My friend, I am not cheating you. You agreed to do a day's work for one silver coin, didn't you? Now take your pay and go home. If I want to give this person who was hired last as much as I gave you, don't I have the right to do as I wish with my money? Or are you envious because I am generous?
Jesus	So those who are last will be first, and those who are first will be last.

The Wedding Feast
Matthew 22:1-14

(Jesus is at the far side. King and Servants are at one side. Guests are at the other side.)

Jesus   The kingdom of heaven is like this. Once there was a king who prepared a wedding feast for his son.

King   *(to Servants 1, 2)*
Go, tell the people invited to our wedding feast to come now.

(Servants 1, 2 go to Guests.)

Servant 1   Come. It's time for the wedding feast at the palace.

Guest 1   I don't feel like going today.

Servant 2   What about you?

Guest 2   We're too busy.

(Servants return to King.)

Servant 1   Your Highness, the guests do not want to come.

King   Hmmm. Maybe they didn't understand.
(to Servants 3, 4)
Come here. Go to my guests. Tell them my banquet is ready now. My best cattle have been butchered. Everything is ready. Come to the wedding feast.

(King, Servants 1, 2 exit. Servants 3, 4 go to Guests.)

Servant 3   The king has this message for you My banquet is ready now. My best cattle have been butchered. Everything is ready. Come to the wedding feast.

Guest 1   *(leaving)*
So long. I'm going to my farm.

Guest 2   *(leaving)*
I have to get to my store.

(Guests 3, 4 grab Servants 3, 4 and beat them to death.)

Guest 3   There. I don't think they'll ever bother anyone again.

(Guests exit.)

Jesus	When the king heard that his servants had been killed, he sent his soldiers to kill the murderers and burn down their city. Then he called for his servants again.
	(Persons 1, 2, 3 enter and go to the far side of stage. King, Servants 1, 2 enter.)
King	*(to Servants 1, 2)* My wedding feast is ready, but the people I invited did not deserve it. So go out into the streets and invite everyone you can find, good or bad.
Servants	Yes, Your Highness. *(Servants go to Persons 1, 2, 3.)*
Servant 1	*(to Person 1)* Come to the King's wedding feast.
Servant 2	*(to Person 2)* Stop your gambling a while and come to the palace for a feast.
Servant 1	*(to Person 3)* You're invited to a royal wedding feast.
	(All move to palace, including Man.)
King	Welcome. Welcome to our feast. Come in. *(King walks among people.)* Ah, it's good to have the hall filled. *(Sees Man without a wedding garment.)*
King	*(to Man)* Friend, how is it that you came in here without a wedding garment?
	(Man is silent.)
King	*(to Servants 1, 2)* Tie him up hand and foot and throw him into the darkness outside. There he will cry and gnash his teeth.
	(Servants take Man out.)
Jesus	Many are invited, but few are chosen.

A House Built on Rock

Matthew 7:24-27   Luke 6:47-49

Jesus   Two men were building houses.

(Man 1 is digging. Man 2 comes to him.)

Man 2   Hey, are you still digging? My house is almost finished, and I started the same time you did.

Man 1   Well, I'm laying a foundation. I want my house to be founded on rock.

Man 2   Why bother? My house is built on sand and it looks great, if I do say so myself.

Man 1   I think my extra time and effort will pay off someday.

Man 2   Good luck.

(Man 1 and Man 2 set chairs some distance apart and sit down.)

Jesus   The two men were in their finished houses when a fierce storm arose. The rain poured down, flood waters rose, and the wind howled.
(sounds of a storm)

Man 2   *(jumping up)*
Oh, no! The walls are shaking. My house is going to collapse. I better get out. *(Runs outside and turns to watch house.)* There it goes!

(Man 1 and Man 2 put their hands over their ears. Sound of house falling.)

Man 1   What was that?

Man 2   Now the flooded river is carrying away every piece. I'm ruined!

(Goes to home of Man 1 and pounds on door.)
Help! Help!

Man 1   What's wrong?

Man 2   My house is completely ruined. Can I stay with you for a while?

Jesus   Anyone who hears my words and obeys them is like a wise man who built his house on rock.

The Sower

Matthew 13:3-9, 18-23   Mark 4:2-9, 14-20   Luke 8:4-8, 11-15

(Jesus and Crowd are off to the side. Thorns are stooping in place. Three Good Seeds offstage have three, six, and ten ears of corn respectively, but out of sight.)

Jesus   *(to Crowd)*
One day a farmer went out to sow some seeds.

(Farmer enters followed by nine Seeds. He takes the first three pairs of Seeds by the hand and flings them to their places. The three Good Seeds are flung together last. The Seeds stoop on the ground. Farmer exits.)

Jesus   *(pointing to Seeds on path)*
Some seeds fell on the path. The birds came and ate them up.

(Birds fly in and take away two Seeds on path.)

Jesus   *(pointing to Seeds on rocky ground)*
Other seeds fell on rocky ground where they had little soil and water. They sprang up right away since the soil wasn't deep.

(Two Seeds stand.)

Jesus   But as soon as the sun came up...

(Sun shines.)

Jesus   They were scorched and, not having any roots, they withered away.

(Seeds sink to ground.)

Jesus   *(pointing to Seeds in thorns)*
 Other seeds fell among thorns. The thorns grew up and choked them, and they produced no crops.

(Thorns and Seeds rise. Thorns wind arms around necks of Seeds. Seeds fall to ground.)

Jesus   *(pointing to Three Good Seeds)*
Still other seeds fell on rich soil and, growing tall and strong, produced their crop.

(Good Seeds stand, smile, and flex arms.)

Jesus   Some thirty.

(One Good Seed holds out three ears.)

Jesus   Some sixty.

(One Good Seed holds out six ears.)

Jesus   Even a hundredfold.

(One Good Seed holds out ten ears. Farmer returns with basket and gathers corn from Three Good Seeds.)

Jesus   Listen, anyone who has ears to hear. What the sower is sowing is the word. The seed on the edge of the path *(walks to where they were and gestures)* are people who hear the word, but Satan comes and carries it away.

Those who received the seed on rocky ground *(moves to rocky ground and gestures)* are those who first hear the word with joy and believe for awhile. But they have no root in them. If a trial comes or some persecution because of the word, they fall away.

Then there are those who receive the word in thorns. *(Moves to Thorns and gestures.)* These, too, have heard the word, but the worries and riches and pleasures of life choke the word, so they produce nothing.

(Moves to Good Seeds.) And there are those who have received the seed in rich soil. They hear the word and accept it and yield a harvest thirty, sixty, and a hundredfold.

The Good Samaritan

Luke 10:25-37

(Jesus and Crowd are at the side. Teacher of the Law enters and comes to Jesus.)

Teacher of the Law   Master, what must I do to receive eternal life?

Jesus   What do the Scriptures say? What do you read there?

Teacher of the Law   You shall love the Lord your God with all your heart, with all your being, and with all your strength, and with all your mind, and your neighbor as yourself.

Jesus   You are right. Do this and you will live.

Teacher of the Law   But who is my neighbor?

Jesus   There was a man on his way down from Jerusalem to Jericho who was attacked by robbers. They took all he had, beat him, and left him half dead.

(Man walks alone. Robbers "beat" him, take his money, and leave him lying on the ground.)

Jesus   A priest came by.

(Priest enters, sees Man, moves to other side of road, and continues on.)

Jesus   A Levite also came there.

(Levite enters, sees Man, moves to other side of road, and continues on.)

Jesus   But a Samaritan who was traveling that way also came upon the man.

(Samaritan enters and stops next to Man.)

Samaritan   Poor fellow. He looks like one of our enemies, a Jewish man. Some oil and wine should help. *(Rubs oil and wine on Man. Takes out cloth and ties it around Man's head.)*

Jesus   The Samaritan lifted the victim onto his own animal and brought him to an inn where he cared for him all night.

(Samaritan helps Man up. They exit. Innkeeper enters.)

Jesus	The next morning the Samaritan went to the innkeeper.
	(Samaritan enters.)
Samaritan	*(giving money to Innkeeper)* Here are two silver pieces for that man I brought in. Take care of him. If you spend more than what I have given you, I will repay you on my way back.
Jesus	Which of the three travelers do you think was neighbor to the man attacked by robbers?
Teacher of the Law	The one who treated him with mercy.
Jesus	Go and do the same.

The Persistent Friend

Luke 11:5-8

(Jesus is off to the side with Disciples. Sam is seated on left side. Friend and Children are sleeping on the floor in the center.)

(Traveler enters and knocks at Sam's house.)

Traveler   Sam, Sam. It's me, Joseph.

Sam   *(going to door)*
What a surprise! It's good to see you, old friend. Come in.

Traveler   Sorry it's so late. I never thought I'd be getting here at midnight.

Sam   No problem. Just have a seat. I'll be back in a minute.

(Traveler sits. Sam goes to Friend's house and knocks.)

Sam   Friend, are you awake?

Friend   *(sitting up and rubbing eyes)*
Huh? Who's there?

Sam   It's me. Lend me three loaves of bread. A friend of mine on a journey has just arrived at my house, and I have no food to offer him.

Friend   Leave me alone. The door has already been locked, and my family and I are in bed. I can't get up to give you anything.

Sam   Please—just this once.

Friend   Don't bother me!

Sam   Friend, what am I to do if you don't help me?

Friend   Oh, all right. How many loaves do you want?

Sam   Three.

(Friend gets loaves, unbolts door, and hands them to Sam.)

Sam   Thanks so much.

Jesus   *(to Disciples)*
I say to you, ask and you shall receive, seek and you shall find, knock and the door will be opened to you.

The Rich Fool
Luke 12:16- 21

(Rich Man is center of stage. Jesus stands to the side.)

Jesus   There was a rich man who had a good harvest.

(Servant enters.)

Servant   Sir, you have never had such good crops.

(Man rubs hands together greedily.)

Servant   Acres and acres of land are ready to be harvested, but the workers will never fit all the grain into the bins.

Rich Man   Wonderful! Go now and let me think.

(Servant leaves.)

Rich Man   What shall I do? I have no place to store my harvest. *(Paces floor, thinking.)* I know! *(Snaps fingers.)* I will tear down my barns and build larger ones where I will store all my grain and my goods. Then I will say to myself,"You have plenty of good things for years to come. Relax, eat, drink, and enjoy yourself."

God's Voice   You fool!

(Man gasps.)

God's Voice   This very night you will have to give up your life. Then who will get this piled-up wealth of yours?

Jesus   This is how it is with those who store up riches for themselves instead of growing rich in what matters to God.

The Barren Fig Tree

Luke 13:6-9

(Jesus is off to the side. The Gardener is some distance from the tree.)

Jesus   A man had a fig tree growing in his orchard, and he came looking for fruit on it.

(Man enters and searches tree for fruit.)

Jesus   But he did not find any.

(Man shakes head.)

Man   *(calling to Gardener)*
Gardener, look here. For three years now I have come to look for fruit on this fig tree and found none. Cut it down. Why should it use up the soil?

Gardener   Sir, leave it one more year. I will hoe around it and fertilize it. Maybe it will bear fruit next year. If not, then you can cut it down.

Man   All right.

The Crafty Steward

Luke 16:1-9

(Rich Man is seated at desk. Reporter enters.)

Reporter Excuse me, sir. I think you should know that the fellow who is managing your property is wasting it.

Rich Man Thank you for the tip. Please have him come here.

(Reporter leaves. Enters with Steward.)

Rich Man What is this I hear about you? Draw up an account of your service, for you can no longer be my steward.

(Rich Man exits.)

Steward What shall I do, now that my employer has fired me? I cannot dig ditches. I am not strong enough. I am ashamed to go begging. Ah, I know what I will do. It's a way to make sure that when I am unemployed people will welcome me into their homes. Messenger!

(Messenger enters.)

Steward Have Jonah and Matthew come here.

(Messenger exits. Debtors 1, 2 enter.)

Steward *(to Debtor 1)*
How much do you owe my master?

Debtor 1 One hundred jars of olive oil.

Steward *(giving him a scroll)*
Take your invoice, sit down, and quickly write one for fifty.

Debtor 1 Say, thanks!

(Debtor 1 sits and writes, then exits.)

Steward *(to Debtor 2)*
How much do you owe?

Debtor 2 A hundred measures of wheat.

Steward *(handing him a scroll)*
Here is your invoice. Make it eighty.

Debtor 2 Great!

(Debtor 2 and Steward exit. Rich Man enters.)

Reporter	Do you know what your clever steward did? He called in your debtors and let them reduce the amount they owed.
Rich Man	Well, I have to give him credit. He certainly is smart.
	(Jesus enters.)
Jesus	The children of this world are cleverer than the children of light in handling their affairs.

The Rich Man and Lazarus

Luke 16:19-31

(Jesus stands off to the side. Lazarus lies at gate. Rich Man is seated at table. Servant stands behind him. Abraham stands at a distance.)

Jesus Once there was a rich man who dressed in purple garments and fine linen. He ate magnificent meals every day. There was also a poor man named Lazarus, who was covered with sores. He lay at the rich man's gate. Dogs even came and licked his sores.

(Servant leaves Rich Man and goes to Lazarus.)

Servant What are you doing here?

Lazarus Food, please. I'm starving. Are there any pieces that have fallen from your master's table?

Servant No. The dogs eat the scraps. *(Exits.)*

Jesus Lazarus died and angels took him to the bosom of Abraham.

(Angels enter and take Lazarus next to Abraham.)

Jesus The rich man also died and was buried.
(Rich Man slumps at table.)
He was punished in the land of the dead.

(Angels take Rich Man some distance from Lazarus and Abraham.)

Rich Man	Father Abraham, have pity on me. Send Lazarus to dip the tip of his finger in water to cool my tongue, for I am in great pain in these flames.
Abraham	My son, remember that in your lifetime you had all good things while Lazarus suffered. Now he is comforted here, while you are in pain. That is not all. Between us there is a great pit. Those who want to cross from our side to yours cannot do so. Nor can anyone cross from your side to ours.
Rich Man	*(pleading)* Father, I beg you then to send Lazarus to my father's house. I have five brothers. Let Lazarus warn them so that they do not end up in this place of pain.
Abraham	They have Moses and the prophets. Let them listen to them.
Rich Man	That is not enough, Father Abraham. But if someone would come to them from the dead, then they would turn from their sins.
Abraham	If they will not listen to Moses and the prophets, they will not be convinced even if someone would rise from the dead.

(Rich Man covers face and groans.)

Rich Man	What a blind fool I was!

The Judge and the Widow

Luke 18:1-8

Jesus	It's important to pray always and not get discouraged. In a certain town there was a judge...
	(Judge passes by, followed by Widow. Person and Visitor stand talking.)
Person	*(to Visitor)* There's our judge. He's a real crook. You can't trust him.
Visitor	I wonder what that woman wants.
Person	She's a widow who lives here, too. The poor woman has been cheated by someone. Everyday she begs the judge to act in her favor. She might as well forget it, if her enemy has bribed the judge.
Woman	*(to Judge)* Sir, give me justice against my enemy.
Judge	You've been bothering me for days now. When will you stop?
Woman	When you stand up for my rights.
Judge	*(sighs)* All right. All right. I'll take care of your case tomorrow.
Woman	*(leaving)* Thank you.
Judge	*(shrugging)* Even though I don't respect God or any human being, I will judge in her favor. If I don't, she will keep coming and pester me to death.
Jesus	Won't God give justice to his chosen people who call out to him day and night? Will he be slow to answer them?

The Pharisee and the Tax Collector
Luke 18:9-14

(Jesus and Crowd are off to the side.)

Jesus   Some people are proud of their virtue and look down on every-one else. Once two people went up to the temple to pray. One was a Pharisee, and the other was a tax collector.

(Pharisee enters, faces audience, arms raised and head un-bowed. The Tax Collector enters and stays far back and to the side. He kneels and keeps his head and eyes down.)

Pharisee   I thank you, God, that I am not greedy, unjust, and adulterous like other people, or even like this tax collector here *(gestures to Tax Collector)*. I fast twice a week. I pay tithes on all I get.

Tax Collector   *(beating breast)*
O God, be merciful to me, a sinner.

Jesus   *(pointing to Tax Collector)*
This man, I tell you, went home from the temple at rights with God. The other did not. For everyone who exalts himself will be humbled, but the one who humbles himself will be exalted.

The Unforgiving Servant
Matthew 18:21-35

(Jesus is off to side. King is seated in center with scroll.)

(Peter enters and goes to Jesus.)

Peter   Lord, if my brother keeps wronging me, how many times do I have to forgive him? Seven times?

Jesus   No, not seven times, but seventy-seven times. The kingdom of God is like this. Once there was a king who decided to check on his servants' accounts.

(King looks at scroll. Servant 1 is brought in by Servants 2, 3.)

Servant 2   Your Highness, here is the man who owes millions of dollars.

Servant 1   Your Excellency, I do not have enough money to pay off this debt.

King   *(to Servants 2, 3)*
Take him away and have him sold as a slave and his wife and children, too. Sell all he owns in order to pay the debt he owes.

Servant 1   *(breaking away and falling on his knees)*
Be patient with me and I will pay back everything.

King   Oh, all right. I'll cancel your debt. Go free.

Servant 1   How can I ever thank you!

(Servants 2, 3 walk to other side. King reads scroll. Servant 4 enters. Servant 1 grabs Servant 4 and starts choking him. Servants 2, 3 watch.)

Servant 1   I loaned you a little money, remember? Pay back what you owe.

Servant 4   *(kneeling)*
Be patient with me and I will pay you back.

Servant 1   No way. You're going to jail until you pay your debt.

(Servant 1 takes Servant 4 out.)

Servant 2   *(to Servant 3)*
How can he do that when the king just cancelled his own debt?

(Servants 2, 3 go to King.)

Servant 3   Your Highness, the servant whose debt you cancelled is a rat.

Servant 2   He is taking one of your men to jail because he owes him a few dollars.

King   Call him here.

(Servants 2, 3 exit and return with Servant 1.)

King   *(to Servant 1, angrily)*
You wicked servant! I cancelled your entire debt, because you begged me to. You should have had pity on your fellow servant, just as I had pity on you.
(to Servants 2, 3)
Take him out of my sight. Let him suffer in jail until he pays back the whole amount.

(Servants 2, 3 take out Servant 1.)

Jesus   That is how my Father in heaven will treat you, unless you forgive your brothers and sisters from your heart.

The Two Sons

Matthew 21:28-32

(Jesus is off to the side with the Religious Leaders. Sons 1, 2 are some distance apart.)

Jesus   What do you think of this? There was once a man who had two sons. One day he went to the older son.

(Father enters and goes to Son 1.)

Father   Son, go and work in the vineyard today.

Son 1   I don't want to.

(Father leaves.)

Son 1   *(to self)*
Now why did I say no? Here my father needs help and I have time. I think I'll go work in the vineyard after all.

(Son 1 leaves. Father enters and goes to Son 2.)

Father   Son, go and work in the vineyard today.

Son 2   Yes, sir.

(Father exits.)

Son 2   *(to self)*
I think I'll go see my friend Jacob. I'm sure Father doesn't really need me in the vineyard.

(Son 2 exits.)

Jesus   Which of the two sons did what the father wanted?

Religious
Leaders   The older one.

Jesus   I tell you, tax collectors and prostitutes are going into the kingdom of God ahead of you. For John the Baptist came to you showing you the right path and you did not believe him. But the tax collectors and the prostitutes believed him. Even when you saw this, you did not change your minds and believe.

The Ten Bridesmaids

Matthew 25:1-13

(Jesus and Crowd are off to the side. The Wise and Foolish Bridesmaids are together, the Wise ones with large flames in their torches and the Foolish with small flames.)

Jesus The kingdom of heaven will be like this. Ten bridesmaids went out with lamps to welcome the bridegroom to his wedding feast.

Wise Bridesmaid 1 There's no sign of him yet. I'm glad I brought extra oil along to keep my lamp burning.

Wise Bridesmaids 2,3,4,5 Me too.

Foolish Bridesmaid 1 I hope he comes soon. I didn't bring any extra oil.

Foolish Bridesmaids 2, 3, 4, 5 Me either.

Wise Bridesmaid 2 We might as well sit while we're waiting.

(Ten Bridesmaids sit down and set their lamps on the ground.)

Foolish Bridesmaid 2 *(yawning)* I'm so tired.

(Ten Bridesmaids nod and then fall asleep.)

Announcer's Voice The bridegroom is here. Come out to meet him.

(Ten Bridesmaids jump up and pick up their lamps.)

Wise Bridesmaid 3 It's midnight already.

(Five Wise Bridesmaids pour oil into their lamps.)

Foolish Briesmaid 3 Give us some of your oil.

Foolish Bridesmaid 4 Our lamps are going out.

Wise *Bridesmaid 4*	No, for there may not be enough for you and us.
Wise *Bridesmaid 5*	You better go to someone who sells it and buy yourselves some.
	(Five Foolish Bridesmaids exit. Bridegroom enters with Announcer and Servant. Wise Bridesmaids cheer.)
Bridegroom	Come in. Come in. *(to Servant)* Bar the door.
	(All go through doorway. Servant bars the door. Foolish Bridesmaids return.)
Foolish *Bridesmaid 5*	*(pounding on door)* Lord, Lord.
Foolish *Bridesmaid 1*	Open the door for us.
Bridegroom	I tell you I do not know you.
	(Five Foolish Bridesmaids exit.)
Jesus	Stay awake because you do not know the day or the hour.

The Three Servants and the Money

Matthew 25:14-30   Luke 19:11-27

(Jesus is off to the side with the Crowd. Man has three bags: 5000, 2000, and 1000. Servants stand in background. Banker stands by Bank sign.)

Jesus   The coming of the kingdom is like this. A man about to go on a journey entrusted his property to his servants according to their ability.

Man   Come here.

(Servants go to Man.)

Man   As you know, I'm going on a long trip. While I'm away, I'd like you to take care of my money. *(Hands 5000 bag to Servant 1.)* Here are 5000 silver pieces for you. *(Hands 2000 bag to Servant 2.)* Here are 2000 for you. *(Hands 1000 bag to Servant 3.)* And here are 1000 for you. I expect each of you to do your best.

(Man exits. Servants 1, 2 go to Banker. Servant 3 takes shovel and goes in the opposite direction.)

Servant 1   *(to Banker)*
I would like to invest these 5000 silver pieces.

Banker   *(taking bag)*
Wonderful.

Servant 2   *(to Banker)*
I would like to invest these 2000 silver pieces.

Banker   *(taking bag)*
Yes, sir.

(Servants 1, 2 and Banker exit.)

Servant 3   *(to self while digging)*
I'll hide the master's money so no one can steal it.

(Servant 3 exits.)

Jesus   After a long time the master returned.

(Man enters. Shortly after, Servant 1 enters with two bags of 5000.)

Man   Well, give me a report on my funds.

Servant 1   Sir, you gave me 5000. I have made 5000 more.

Man   Well done, my good and faithful servant. Since you were faithful in small matters, I will put you in charge of greater. Come, share your master's joy.

(Servant 2 enters with two bags of 2000.)

Servant 2   Sir, you gave me 2,000. I have made 2,000 more.

Man   Well done, my good and faithful servant. Since you were faithful in small matters, I will put you in charge of greater. Come, share your master's joy.

(Servant 3 enters with bag of 1,000.)

Servant 3   Sir, I knew you were a hard man. You reap where you did not plant, and you gather crops where you did not scatter seed. I was afraid, so I went off and buried your money in the ground. Here it is.

Man   You worthless, lazy servant. So you knew I reap where I did not plant and gather crops where I did not scatter seed? Well, then, you should have deposited my money in the bank so that I could have got it back with interest on my return.

(to Servant 2)
Take the thousand away from him and give it to the man with 10,000. Those who have will be given more until they are rich, but those who have nothing will lose even the little they have.

(Servant 2 takes bag from Servant 3 and gives it to Servant 1.)

Man   As for this useless servant, throw him into the darkness outside where he will cry and grind his teeth.

(Servants 1, 2 take hold of Servant 3 and exit.)

DIRECTOR'S HANDBOOK

TIPS FOR PUTTING ON PLAYLETS

1. Make a copy of the playlet for each participant who has a speaking part or a major role. Highlight, or have the students highlight, all of their parts, including stage directions.

2. If you wish, make an identification sign or headband for each character.

3. Allow as many students as possible to participate in the playlet. Cast names marked + in the Director's Handbook can be adjusted to the size of your class.

4. If you wish, prepare the props that are suggested for some playlets. Printed signs indicating the setting would also be helpful, particularly if the location changes during the play. Pictures of scenery drawn on the blackboard could serve as the backdrop for the playlet.

5. List the characters on the board so that students can sign for parts before class. They might have time to practice and even to memorize their lines.

6. Actors could rehearse together during class while the rest of the students are engaged in another activity. A teacher aide might take the group to another room for practice.

7. Encourage the participants

   to look up from their scripts as much as possible

   to speak so as to be heard and understood

   to avoid having their backs to the audience

   to use expression in interpreting their lines

   to be creative in adding movements and gestures.

8. Before the playlet begins, have the characters introduce themselves to the audience, especially if they are not wearing identification.

9. Compliment the group or individuals for a job well done.

10. Make sure that each student has a speaking role sometime, and not always just a member of the crowd.

Caution: Avoid putting on a playlet only for the sake of putting on a playlet. With no proper introduction or follow-up, a playlet is a waste of time instead of a meaningful educational experience.

WATER INTO WINE

John 2:1-11
Second Sunday of the Year C

CAST	PROPS
Narrator	Tureen or pitcher
Bride	Headwaiter
Jesus	Ladle
Groom	Mug
Mary	Red punch
Disciples 1, 2	or Kool-Aid
Servants 1, 2	
Guests +	

THEMES
Identity of Jesus, Mary,
Sacrament of Marriage

COMMENTS
According to John's gospel, changing water into wine by a word was the first sign that Jesus worked to reveal his identity. Both a wedding feast and an abundance of wine are symbols of the messianic age. Jesus is the Messiah, the one who announces and makes present the reign of God. The water Jesus used for the miracle was reserved for ceremonial washings. The wine that he produces is not only plentiful, but excellent, as the headwaiter attests. In Jesus is the fullness that satisfies every living creature.

The intercessory role of Mary is highlighted in this miracle. She relies on her son to help when the wine runs low, and as a result the newlyweds are spared embarrassment. Jesus' words to her are mysterious. He addresses her as "woman," just as he does later as she stands at the foot of the cross. Perhaps this title is a sign that she is a new Eve who brings forth new life as the church does. The "hour" that Jesus speaks of is his glorification, the Paschal Mystery that achieves salvation. The miracle of wine, which occurs "on the third day," obviously foreshadows that hour.

POINTS FOR DISCUSSION
- The abundance and excellence of what Jesus provides
- The willingness and ability of Jesus to help us in our needs
- Mary's part in salvation.
- How Mary intercedes for us
- Favorite prayers and signs of devotion to Mary
- The blessings of Jesus on a wedding celebration

CALMING OF THE STORM

Matthew 8:23-27 Mark 4:35-41
Luke 8:22-25
Twelfth Sunday of the Year B

CAST	PROPS
Narrator	4 or more pairs of
Jesus	chairs, one behind
Disciples 1, 2, 3,	the other for a boat
4, 5, 6 +	Cushion
	Soundmakers for
	thunder and waves

THEMES
Faith: need for faith, humanness of Jesus, identity of Jesus

COMMENTS
This miracle account reveals more clearly

the identity of Jesus. He is so human that fatigue causes him to sleep through a bad storm. Yet he is able to subdue the wind and waves by a word. To the Jewish people the sea was considered life-threatening, a symbol of evil. In Hebrew Scriptures, the act of creation is described as God's conquest over the sea. Consequently, when Jesus masters the sea, he manifests divine power. He is raised up out of his sleep and conquers evil as he one day will be raised up out of his tomb and triumph over evil forever. The story also calls for deeper faith on our part. After rebuking the sea, Jesus chides the disciples for their lack of faith. If we believe in Jesus, we trust him to care for us through all the storms of life, even when he appears to be sleeping.

POINTS FOR DISCUSSION
- Why Jesus was tired
- Signs of Jesus' humanness
- Storms we might have to weather
- Times when Jesus gave us strength
- Reasons for trusting Jesus

THE MULTIPLICATION OF LOAVES
||||||||||||||||||||||||||||||||||||||||||||||||||||||||||||||||||||||||||||||||||||||||
Matthew 14:13-21 Mark 6:30-44
Luke 9:10-17 John 6:1-15
Eighteenth Sunday of the Year A
Seventeenth Sunday of the Year B

CAST	PROPS
Narrator	Five paper loaves
Jesus	Two paper fish
Peter	Three baskets
Andrew	
Philip	

Boy
Persons 1, 2
Crowd +
Other Apostles +

THEMES
Eucharist, ministry, use of gifts

COMMENTS
This miracle account strikes familiar chords in Jewish and Christian hearts. It recalls the Exodus during which God fed the people of Israel with manna and quail in the wilderness. It brings to mind the bread miracles of the prophets Elijah (1 Kings 17:2-6) and Elisha (2 Kings 4:42-44). It presents Jesus as the shepherd who spreads a banquet before us. The story also looks to the future. It prefigures the Last Supper, the Christian eucharistic celebration, and the messianic banquet. In John's gospel the story is followed by the discourse on the Bread of Life, which serves to heighten the eucharistic dimension of the miracle.

Jesus has compassion on the hungry crowd. He takes the little food the apostles provide and makes it more to feed the people. His actions are described by the same words used in the account of the institution of the eucharist. At the end when everyone is satisfied, there are twelve baskets left over. Twelve symbolizes fullness.

This miracle is the Parable of the Leaven in action. The bread distributed through the crowd to nourish it is like the growth and blessings of God's kingdom.

POINTS FOR DISCUSSION
- The superabundance that Jesus provides us
- How this miracle is a preparation for and symbol of the eucharist

- The ways that Jesus has the apostles help him minister to the people
- Examples of how we can satisfy one another's hunger
- Some gifts we might let God use for God's work
- How in God we find all that we long for

THE LARGE CATCH OF FISH

Luke 5:1-11
Fifth Sunday of the Year C

CAST	PROPS
Narrator	Two sets of chairs
Jesus	for two boats
James	Two nets
John	
Simon	
Peter	
Andrew	
Partner	
Persons 1, 2 +	
Crowd +	

THEMES
Discipleship, Peter

COMMENTS
In Luke the lake is a place for manifestations of power. This particular miracle happens when the fishermen trust Jesus, a non-fisherman, to put out their nets once more. Although they had caught nothing all night, suddenly there is an overwhelming number of fish available. In response to the miracle of the large catch, Peter falls to his knees before Jesus. All the fishermen, sensing that they are in the presence of the divine, leave everything to follow him.

It is Peter's boat from which the Lord speaks. It is Peter who first acknowledges Jesus' greatness and his own unworthiness. Also, the Lord addresses the words "You will be catching people" to Peter alone, using the singular. These features indicate Peter's vocation of leadership in the church. The verb used for "will be catching" implies that it will be lifelong.

POINTS FOR DISCUSSION
- The power of Jesus over people and over nature
- The rewards of doing what Jesus advises
- Signs in the story of Peter's special role in the church
- What being "fishers of people" entails
- The teamwork needed on the part of Jesus and the fishermen in order to catch the fish
- How we can be recognized as followers of Jesus

WALKING ON THE SEA

|||||||||||||||||||||||||||||||||||||||||||||||||||||||||||||||||||||

Matthew 14:22-33 Mark 6:45-52
John 6:16-21
Nineteenth Sunday of the Year A

CAST	PROPS
Narrator	Pairs of chairs in a
Jesus	row for boat
Disciple 1, 2, 3, +	
Peter	
Crowd +	

THEMES
Faith: need for faith, identity of Jesus, Peter

COMMENTS
Jesus' power over the sea signified divinity to the Jewish people. This miracle recalls the Exodus during which God saved the Israelites by mighty deeds, such as leading them safely through the Reed Sea. The story takes place on Lake Gennesaret, which is subject to sudden storms. Jesus walks on the surface of the lake, enables Peter to walk on it, and quiets the wind and the waves. This miracle, therefore, is a revelation of Christ's divinity to the apostles. He even identifies himself by saying, "It is I," which is comparable to "I am," the name Yahweh revealed to Moses.

If the apostles in their boat stand for the church, the story teaches that Jesus is present to assist his church through any storm. In Matthew's account Peter is singled out, a sign of his responsibility in the church. As long as he has faith and has his hand in Jesus' hand, he is able to do what he should as a leader.

POINTS FOR DISCUSSION
• The signs of Jesus' divinity
• Storms we might have to weather in life
• How Jesus reaches his hand out to support us in difficult times
• Ways Jesus is present
• The care of Jesus for his church

THE TAX MONEY IN THE FISH

|||||||||||||||||||||||||||||||||||||||||||||||||||||||||||||||||||||||||||||||||||

Matthew 17:24-27

CAST	PROPS
Narrator	Paper fish with
Jesus	penny taped to it
Peter	String tied to pole
Tax Collectors 1, 2	

THEMES
Obedience to laws, Peter, virtue

COMMENTS
Every adult male over nineteen was obliged to pay a half-shekel temple tax annually. Just as Roman citizens were exempt from paying Roman taxes, we may think of Jesus and the apostles, as members of the kingdom of heaven, as exempt from the temple tax. But so as not to give scandal, Jesus arranges to pay the tax for himself and for Peter. This story might have been used to settle a problem of the early church regarding the temple tax.

POINTS FOR DISCUSSION
• The humor in Jesus sending a fisherman to fish for the tax money
• What is meant by scandal?

- Church regulations that we are obliged to follow
- How our monetary offerings support the church

THE SECOND LARGE CATCH OF FISH

||||||||||||||||||||||||||||||||||||||||||||||||||||||||||||||||||||||||||||||||

John 21:1-14
Third Sunday of Easter C

CAST	PROPS
Narrator	Eight chairs in pairs
Jesus	for boat
Peter	Cloak
Thomas	Bread
Nathanael	A few fish
James	Net
John	
Disciples 1, 2	

THEMES
Easter/eternal life, identity of Jesus, ministry

COMMENTS
This miracle story has eucharistic overtones. It resembles the multiplication of loaves and fish that also occurred on the shore of the Sea of Tiberias (Lake Gennesaret.) The apostles catch nothing all night. Then when they cast their net to the lucky side of the boat at the direction of a man on shore, they make an enormous catch. With this miracle of abundance Peter recognizes that the stranger is the Lord. Peter dons his cloak because Jewish etiquette required that greetings be made in proper attire. Then in a typically spontaneous way he jumps overboard and swims to Jesus.

Although Jesus has been cooking fish, he asks for some of the apostles' fish. This act symbolizes the apostles' share in his mission. Why the gospel states the precise number of fish caught remains a mystery.

The large number may suggest the universal dimension of the church's ministry. A simpler explanation is that the apostles, like any fishermen proud and excited by a huge catch, counted the fish and remembered the large number.

Because this is a post-resurrection appearance of Jesus, the apostles naturally are awed and puzzled by the mystery of his presence with them. They are slow to identify him and do not ask him to confirm that he is the Lord.

POINTS FOR DISCUSSION
- How the story is like the multiplication of loaves and fishes
- Other things that Jesus provides in super-abundance
- Ways we share in Christ's mission
- How to recognize the Lord

A POSSESSED MAN

|||||||||||||||||||||||||||||||||||||||||||||||||||||||||||||||||||||||||||||||||||||

Mark 1:21-28 Luke 4:31-37
Fourth Sunday of the Year B

CAST

Narrator
Jesus
Man
Persons 1, 2
Crowd +

THEME
Identity of Jesus

COMMENTS
In the gospels of Mark and Luke, exorcism is the first miracle that Jesus worked. An exorcism is an appropriate beginning to his ministry, since it signals Jesus' ultimate victory over evil. Demons are powerless before him, even if, like the ones in this miracle, they know his name (a way to have magical power over an enemy).

At Jesus' words a struggle ensues that underlines the gravity of the man's situation. Whether truly possessed or suffering from a disease attributed to demons, the man regains his health. Once more he is welcome in society and in the synagogue.

POINTS FOR DISCUSSION
• What possession and exorcism are
• How sin separates us from others
• Why Jesus is unique
• How we can rely on Jesus in our struggle against evil

DEMONS SENT INTO SWINE

||||||||||||||||||||||||||||||||||||||||||||||||||||||||||||||||||||||||||||||||||||||||||||||||||||||

Matthew 8:28-34 Mark 5:1-20
Luke 8:26-39

CAST   PROPS

Narrator   Broken chains
Jesus
Disciples 1, 2
Man
Swineherds 1, 2
Persons 1, 2, 3 +

THEMES
Evangelization, universal salvation

COMMENTS
In this colorful miracle account Jesus saves a Gentile and makes him an evangelist. The possessed man has lived among tombs, the place where demons were believed to live. The evil that possesses him causes him to hurt himself. When Jesus arrives, the demons, as usual, recognize him as the Son of God. Jesus learns their name, which was thought at that time to give him power over them. He sends "Legion" into swine, which immediately rush into the sea. The earth is no place for demons when Jesus is there.

The cured man sits at Jesus' feet like a student. Ironically, the people, seeing the man sane again, fear Jesus' power and ask him to leave. When the man begs to go with him, Jesus tells him to spread the news of his healing.

POINTS FOR DISCUSSION
• How people at that time attributed certain illnesses to demons
• How sin and evil lead to self-destruction
• The power of God over all evil

- Why people may reject Jesus
- Our call to proclaim the good things God has done for us

POINTS FOR DISCUSSION
- What possession and exorcism mean
- What Jesus' miracles say about him
- How we can bring people who are under Satan's rule to Jesus for help by our prayer and actions
- Sickness and suffering as signs of evil in the world

A POSSESSED, BLIND, MUTE MAN

Matthew 12:22-28 Luke 11:14-20

CAST

Jesus
Possessed Man
Persons 1, 2, 3, 4
Pharisees 1, 2
Crowd +

THEME
Identity of Jesus

COMMENTS
The exorcisms of Jesus are not like those of common magicians who were thought to act with the help of demons. His exorcisms were accomplished by a simple command, sometimes combined with a touch. The point of this account is that Jesus' actions signal the presence of the reign of God. He works not by the power of Beelzebul, an evil spirit, but by the power of the Spirit of God.

The miracle Jesus works for the suffering man doesn't satisfy the Pharisees. When they request a miracle, they mean one in line with their concept of a messiah: a military victory. Jesus doesn't grant their request. The arguments of Jesus against the accusations of these Pharisees are logical. He wins the case.

PETER'S MOTHER-IN-LAW

Matthew 8:14-15 Mark 1:29-31
Luke 4:38-39
Fifth Sunday of the Year B

CAST	PROPS
Narrator	Loaf of bread
Jesus	Mat, carpet or table
James	for bed
John	
Peter	
Andrew	
Mother-in-Law	
Peter's Wife	

THEME
Peter

COMMENTS
When friends intercede for Peter's mother-in-law, Jesus heals her. Homey details make this miracle story seem like an eyewitness account. On a deeper level certain features hold a message for Christians. Jesus "rebukes" the fever as though conquering a demon. The mother-in-law is "raised up," an expression that points to his resurrection. After she is restored, the

woman waits on the people gathered there. An implication is that we who have been saved by Christ have a responsibility to serve.

POINTS FOR DISCUSSION
- People who are in need of our prayers, especially our own family members
- How Jesus has saved us
- Ways we can minister to others in our family, neighborhood, and school
- How to show love and care for the sick

clean. He then has the leper comply with the Mosaic law that requires that a leper with an offering appear before a priest in order to be declared clean. Despite Jesus' orders to keep the miracle quiet, the man spreads the news of his good fortune.

POINTS FOR DISCUSSION
- The disease of leprosy and its restrictions
- How Jesus is Savior in all our needs
- The people are the lepers in our communities and how we can go out to them
- Areas in our lives that need healing

A LEPER

Matthew 8:1-4 Mark 1:40-45 Luke 5:12-15
Sixth Sunday of the Year B

CAST

Narrator
Jesus
Leper
Persons 1, 2

THEME
Evangelization

COMMENTS
The leper's highly contagious skin disease cut him off from the community. He approaches Jesus with faith in his power to heal his leprosy and his loneliness. With pity for the man and anger for the cause of his suffering, Jesus answers his plea to be made clean. Stretching out his hand, a gesture of saving that recalls God's help during the Exodus, Jesus heals the leper. By touching him, Jesus makes himself un-

THE PARALYTIC

Matthew 9:1-8 Mark 2:1-12 Luke 5:17-26
Seventh Sunday of the Year B

CAST

CAST	PROPS
Narrator	Mat or carpeting
Jesus	
Paralyzed Man	
Friends 1, 2, 3, 4	
Teachers of the Law 1, 2	
Persons 1, 2	

THEMES
Forgiveness of sin, sin

COMMENTS
Jesus responds to the plight of the paralytic because of his faith and the faith of his friends. In their desire to reach Jesus, they come in through the roof. The entrance was easily made because the roof was probably just clay and straw.

In curing the man the first step Jesus takes is to forgive his sins. The paralytic's

act of faith implied repentance. Once the root of all evil has been destroyed, Jesus deals with one of its side effects—illness. The story presents the healing as proof that Jesus has divine power and authority to forgive sins. It illustrates that his role as Savior goes beyond the physical.

POINTS FOR DISCUSSION

- How sin is like paralysis
- How friends can bring one another closer to Jesus
- The consequences of sin in the world
- Ways we can receive Jesus' forgiveness today
- Reasons we have to praise and thank God for his goodness

a sheep on a sabbath, certainly it would be lawful to help a human being. Unwilling to admit that good could be performed on the sabbath, the Pharisees are silent and incur Jesus' anger for their hard hearts. As a result of Jesus' controversial words and actions, these Pharisees begin to plot how to put him to death.

POINTS FOR DISCUSSION

- Parts of our lives that are "withered" and in need of Jesus' healing
- Good acts we could do to make Sunday holy
- Examples of how we could have hard hearts in regard to one of Jesus' teachings
- How the good are sometimes persecuted

THE MAN WITH A WITHERED HAND

Matthew 12:9-14 Mark 3:1-6, Luke 6:6-11
Ninth Sunday of the Year B

CAST

Narrator
Jesus
Man
Pharisees 1, 2, 3
Crowd +

THEMES
Opposition to Jesus, sabbath cures

COMMENTS
Jesus' healing of the man with the withered hand sparks another confrontation with some Pharisees about the sabbath. Jesus points out that if a person could help

THE CENTURION'S SERVANT

Matthew 8:5-13 Luke 7:1-10
Ninth Sunday of the Year C

CAST

Narrator
Jesus
Centurion
Crowd +
Jewish Elder
Messenger

THEMES
Faith: praise of faith, universal salvation

COMMENTS
The focus of this miracle is the Gentile's faith, which results in Jesus curing someone at a distance. The centurion's young

slave, whom he loves, is gravely ill. Wishing to spare Jesus the inconvenience and ritual uncleanness that a visit would cause, the Gentile declares his belief that Jesus has only to speak to perform a miracle. Jesus praises the man and predicts that people from East and West will partake in the feast of the kingdom. Everyone is welcome. The servant is restored to perfect health. The beautiful words of the centurion have been incorporated into our eucharistic liturgy before communion.

POINTS FOR DISCUSSION

• Why the centurion requests that Jesus only speak in order to heal his servant

• Jesus' power and his willingness to answer our prayers

• What is required to join in the feast of heaven

• How we can show faith

• Examples of recent miracles of healing

• Where we might need healing

THE CANAANITE WOMAN

Matthew 15:21-28 Mark 7:24-30
Twentieth Sunday of the Year A

CAST	PROPS
Narrator	Mat or carpeting for
Jesus	bed
Disciples 1, 2	
Woman	
Daughter	

THEMES
Faith: praise of faith, universal salvation

COMMENTS
The theme of universal salvation predominates in this story. Jesus works a miracle for the benefit of a Gentile woman. Moreover, she is identified as one of the Canaanites, whom the Jews at that time considered wicked pagans. As with other cures for Gentiles, Jesus works this one at a distance.

Jesus' first response to the woman's plea seems brusque and even rude. Commentators propose that he might be quoting a proverb. The children are the Jewish people, while the Gentiles are the puppies. The Gentiles were sometimes vulgarly referred to as dogs. The woman's quick retort is witty. Because of it and because of her faith, Jesus in her case extends his ministry to the Gentiles. Both Jews and Gentiles are fed in the Father's house. The church of Jesus is catholic—for all.

POINTS FOR DISCUSSION

• How Jesus is Lord and Savior of all people

• Ways to express gratitude to God for salvation

• Sick people, especially family members, who need our prayers

• The reward for not giving up in praying for an intention

• People we might bring to Jesus

A DEAF MUTE

|||||||||||||||||||||||||||||||||||||||||||||||||||||||||||||||||||||||||

Mark 7:31-37
Twenty-Third Sunday of the Year B

CAST

Narrator
Jesus
Deaf Mute
Persons 1, 2, 3, 4

THEMES
Evangelization, hearing God's word

COMMENTS
Jesus effects the healing of the deaf mute through gestures and a strange word, rituals that were characteristic of contemporary healers including pagan magicians. In those days saliva was believed to have medicinal power. Jesus' intimacy with God is symbolized by his looking up to heaven.

The messianic secret that distinguishes Mark's gospel occurs twice in this miracle account. Jesus calls the man apart from the crowd to cure him. After the miracle he tells the crowd not to speak of it.

An optional "ephphetha" rite is part of our baptism ceremony. The priest or deacon prays that the candidate be open to God's word and proclaim the faith.

POINTS FOR DISCUSSION
- What it must be like to be deaf and to speak with difficulty
- The meaning of the ephphetha ritual in the baptismal ceremony
- When we can hear God's word
- How we show that we are open to God's word
- Ways to spread the Good News

AN EPILEPTIC BOY

|||||||||||||||||||||||||||||||||||||||||||||||||||||||||||||||||||||||||

Matthew 17:14-20 Mark 9:14-29
Luke 9:37-43

CAST

Jesus
Father
Boy
Disciples 1, 2, 3, 4
Crowd +
Person in Crowd

THEME
Faith: need for faith

COMMENTS
This miracle illustrates Jesus' messianic power. It is Jesus, not the apostles, who is strong enough to drive out the demon that possesses the boy. The detailed symptoms emphasize the seriousness of the disease and therefore the greatness of the miracle.

Faith is a key theme in the story. Jesus encourages the father to believe. When Jesus states that anything is possible with faith, the father prays for stronger faith. At the end Jesus explains the unlimited power of faith.

The boy's exorcism symbolizes the resurrection, the sign of Jesus' complete triumph over Satan.

POINTS FOR DISCUSSION
- The disease of epilepsy
- When we might turn to Jesus to save us from evil
- What faith is
- The means we have to strengthen our faith

THE INFIRM WOMAN

Luke 13:10-17

CAST

Narrator
Jesus
Woman
Crowd +
Persons 1, 2
Chief of Synagogue
Opponents +

THEME
Sabbath cures

COMMENTS
In this miracle account Jesus takes the initiative. The woman does not request a cure; nor does she demonstrate faith. Yet Jesus calls her to him to be cured. This sign can be considered an essential part of his teaching in the synagogue. The chief of the synagogue criticizes Jesus indirectly by telling the people not to come to be cured on the sabbath. But Jesus retorts with a new, more humane teaching: Of course, good may be done on the sabbath. God's laws are more reasonable than human laws.

POINTS FOR DISCUSSION
- How to imitate Jesus' regard for the unfortunate and the outcast
- Ways to celebrate the sabbath in order to make it a special day
- Other teachings of Jesus that stress love of neighbor

THE MAN WITH DROPSY

Luke 14:1-6

CAST

Narrator
Jesus
Pharisees 1, 2
Guests 1, 2 +
Man

THEME
Sabbath cures

COMMENTS
Even in the social setting of a banquet, some Pharisees watch Jesus. Aware of their scrutiny, Jesus asks outright if curing on a sabbath is lawful. When the Pharisees do not respond, Jesus heals a man with dropsy. Jesus appeals to the reason of these Pharisees by asking if they would rescue a son or ox from a pit on the sabbath. To this, too, they are silent. They refuse to admit that Jesus is right.

POINTS FOR DISCUSSION
- How we can refuse to act on the truth
- Times it takes courage to do what is right because it means being different
- Healings we have heard about

THE TEN LEPERS

|||||||||||||||||||||||||||||||||||||||||||||||||||||||||||||||||||||||||||||||||||||

Luke 17:11-19
Twenty-Eighth Sunday of the Year C

CAST	PROPS

Narrator   Cane
Jesus
Lepers 1, 2, 3, 4,
5, 6, 7, 8, 9
Samaritan Leper

THEMES

Gratitude, prejudice

COMMENTS

The miracle focuses on the importance of gratitude to God. The faith of the lepers is praiseworthy. They trust in Jesus to deliver them from their dread disease that isolates them and makes them outcasts. He sends them to have their cure verified by the priests. On the way, when the lepers realize they are clean, only one decides to return to thank Jesus for his kindness. The others are either too caught up in their joy to think of returning or they do not wish to spend the time and energy it would cost to return.

The hero of the story, the leper who gave thanks, is a Samaritan, a traditional enemy of the Jewish people. Jesus' attention to lepers and Samaritans illustrates his acceptance of all people.

POINTS FOR DISCUSSION

- Times when we ought to thank God
- Ways to show gratitude to God and to other people
- The lepers and Samaritans in our world who need our acceptance
- The difficulty of doing what is right, if we

are the only ones
- Showing gratitude for health by taking care of our body

BLIND BARTIMAEUS

||||||||||||||||||||||||||||||||||||||||||||||||||||||||||||||||||||||||||||||||||||||||||||||||||||

Matthew 20:29-34 Mark 10:46-52
Luke 18:35-43
Thirtieth Sunday of the Year B

CAST	PROPS

Narrator   Cloak (or jacket)
Jesus
Crowd +
Bartimaeus
Bystanders 1, 2, 3

THEMES

Faith: praise of faith, perseverance in prayer

COMMENTS

In this last miracle story before going to Jerusalem, Jesus lets himself be loudly acclaimed as the Son of David, not by a demon but by a blind beggar. Ironically the blind man recognizes Jesus for who he is. In response to the man's faith, Jesus has pity on him and heals him. Bartimaeus, having been gifted with perfect vision, then follows Jesus as a disciple.

POINTS FOR DISCUSSION

- How faith is a matter of spiritual vision
- The courage and risk involved in going to Jesus
- The kind of messiah Jesus really was in contrast to the kind that the Israelites expected
- What we might beg Jesus for

THE NOBLEMAN'S SON

John 4:46-54

CAST

Narrator
Jesus
Nobleman
Servants 1, 2

THEME
Faith: healings resulting from faith

COMMENTS
The royal official, who probably served Herod, apparently knew of Jesus' power to heal. When his son is very sick, he seeks out Jesus and implores him to come cure him. Jesus warns against a faith based on miracles, but then grants the man's request. The correspondence in time between Jesus' assurance that the boy will live and the boy's actual recovery is proof of the miracle. The sign leads to faith for the man and his whole house.

POINTS FOR DISCUSSION
• Why we believe in Jesus
• Why we can ask Jesus for miracles
• World intentions for which we might pray
• How Jesus' universal love includes the powerful and the weak, the rich and the poor

CURE AT THE POOL AT BETHESDA

John 5:1-18
Twenty-Second Sunday of the Year B

CAST	*PROPS*
Narrator	Mats for the sick
Jesus	
Man	
Pharisees 1, 2	
Sick People +	
Crowd +	

THEMES
Sabbath cures, sin

COMMENTS
Evidently the pool in this miracle was fed by an underground spring with curative powers. John gives it the Hebrew name, Bethesda, which means "house of mercy." Without benefit of the water, but merely by the force of his word, Jesus heals a man who has been paralyzed for thirty-eight years.

A specific law forbade carrying a bed on the sabbath. When the man obeys Jesus, his healer, and carries his mat away, he is rebuked by Pharisees. This leads to further controversy between Jesus and some Pharisees.

When Jesus warns the man not to sin lest something worse will befall him, he is not implying that the man's disease was the result of his sin. Rather, he is referring to the eternal consequences of evil choices.

POINTS FOR DISCUSSION
• The healing power of mineral springs
• How the church exercises the gift of healing today

- The primacy of Jesus' laws over human laws
- How sin and suffering are related
- Ways that a Christian can minister to the sick

THE MAN BORN BLIND

John 9:1-41
Fourth Sunday of Lent A

CAST	PROPS
Narrator	Bowl or pan
Jesus	of water
Mother	
Father	
Man	
Messenger	
Disciples 1, 2	
Pharisees 1, 2	
Neighbors 1, 2, 3 +	

THEMES

Faith: healings resulting from faith, opposition to Jesus, sacrament of baptism, sabbath cures

COMMENTS

This miracle story traces the path of a person who encounters and follows Jesus, the Light. It has a definite sacramental dimension. The beggar has been in darkness from birth until Jesus cures him without being asked. The healing is brought about by "anointing" with mud and washing with water from the pool of Siloam, which means "sent."

Because it is sabbath, some Pharisees

challenge and question the man. Through the process the man who now has sight grows in understanding of Jesus. He defends the one who healed him even when his own parents desert him. His arguments reveal that he sees much more clearly than the blind Pharisees. Unable to disprove the miracle, the Pharisees cast the man out. Eventually, Jesus seeks out the cured man and calls him to the fullness of faith.

POINTS FOR DISCUSSION

- The free gift of faith
- Why Jesus is our light
- The significance of baptism
- The demands of our baptismal commitment
- Times we might have to be strong in declaring our faith in Jesus
- How we can grow in understanding of Jesus

RAISING THE WIDOW'S SON

||||||||||||||||||||||||||||||||||||||||||||||||||||||||||||||||||||||||||||||||||

Luke 7:11-17
Tenth Sunday of the Year C

CAST	PROPS
Narrator	Table or chairs side
Jesus	by side for bier
Followers 1, 2 +	(pallet)
Widow	
Woman	
Son	
Mourners 1, 2 +	
Bearers 1, 2, 3, 4	

THEME
Easter/eternal life

COMMENTS
Jesus fittingly is called Lord here for the first time in Luke's gospel. In this miracle he shows himself master of life and death. Jesus and his crowd of followers encounter a woman at the head of a funeral procession. Burying the dead was an important work of mercy. Even the poorest people hired mourners and musicians for a funeral. Jesus is filled with pity for the mother. She is a widow who has lost her only son. As such she prefigures Mary. Through God's power the widow's son, like Mary's, comes back to life.

Jesus' handing the young man to his mother recalls Elijah's raising of a widow's son (1 Kings 17:8-24). The people who observe the miracle acclaim Jesus as a great prophet like Elijah. Raising the dead is a sign that Jesus is "the one who is to come" (Luke 7:20).

POINTS FOR DISCUSSION
• The compassion of Jesus for the woman
• How the story prefigures Jesus' death
• The signs that Jesus is a great prophet
• How our funeral rites reflect our belief in the resurrection
• Ways we support and comfort others in their grief

RAISING JAIRUS'S DAUGHTER AND HEALING THE SICK WOMAN

||||||||||||||||||||||||||||||||||||||||||||||||||||||||||||||||||||||||||||||||||

Matthew 9:18-26   Mark 5:21-43
Luke 8:40-56
Thirteenth Sunday of the Year B

CAST	PROPS
Jesus	Cloak
Messenger	Mat for bed
Peter	
James	
John	
Jairus	
Woman	
Girl	
Mother	
Mourners 1, 2, 3 +	
Crowd +	
Persons 1, 2	

THEME
Faith: healings resulting from faith

COMMENTS
These two stories of Jesus' healing of women are presented as a unit. The healing of the sick woman is sandwiched within the story of Jairus's daughter. In both accounts faith is underlined. Jairus kneels before Jesus, believing that his touch will cure his daughter. The woman secretly

touches the tassel on Jesus' cloak, believing that this contact would heal her. Both acts of faith are rewarded.

The two miracles point to Jesus as Savior. The woman's condition made her unclean for twelve years; it also made her poor. Jesus was her salvation. The raising of Jairus's daughter from death prefigures Jesus' resurrection. The girl passes from death to new life, and the mourners' wails are in vain.

The cloak Jesus wore had a tassel on each corner as prescribed by law. However, he stepped outside the law when he let the unclean woman touch him and when he touched the girl's corpse. His love goes beyond the law.

POINTS FOR DISCUSSION

- How Jesus treats women at a time when rabbis were not even supposed to address them in public
- Ways that we can show faith
- What Jesus' power over death means for us
- Times when we might look to Jesus for help

THE RAISING OF LAZARUS

John 11:1-44
Fifth Sunday of Lent A

CAST	PROPS
Narrator	Cloths or towels
Jesus	for Lazarus
Disciples 1, 2, 3	Large box or cart
Thomas	
Lazarus	
Martha	
Mary	

Messenger
Mourners +
Men to move stone +

THEMES
Easter/eternal life, humanness of Jesus

COMMENTS
The raising of Lazarus is a preparation for the resurrection of Jesus. When Jesus receives the message that his friend is ill, he does not go to him immediately. Lazarus's death is part of a plan to reveal his power. Then when Jesus arrives, Martha's remark that if he had been there Lazarus would not have died leads to a conversation on the resurrection.

A group is gathered at Lazarus's house because mourning rites usually continued for seven days. Jesus is truly grieved at the death of his friend. He prays aloud so that the people know that the Father sent him. Then at Jesus' command, after being dead four days, Lazarus steps forth and is unbound from his burial cloths. The gospel provides no further details.

Ironically, Jesus' miracle of restoring Lazarus to life precipitates the Pharisees' plot to kill him.

POINTS FOR DISCUSSION

- The human qualities of Jesus revealed in this miracle
- Why Jesus doesn' t go to Lazarus immediately
- How we would have felt on witnessing the miracle
- The deceased among our family and friends for whom we could pray
- Why Christians need not fear death
- How our funeral rites reflect our faith in the resurrection
- How Jesus brings us to life after sin

THE LOST SHEEP

Matthew 18:12-14 Luke 15:3-7
Twenty-Fourth Sunday of the Year C

CAST

Jesus
Shepherd
Sheep +
Lost Sheep
Friends +

THEMES
Forgiveness of sin,
sacrament of reconciliation

COMMENTS
In this parable Jesus compares a sinner to a lost sheep, and God to the concerned shepherd who goes after it. Just as the shepherd misses his stray sheep, God longs to have the sinner safe back home. A lost sheep that has lain down and rolled over is unable to walk. In such "cast sheep" circulation is cut off. The shepherd has to carry the sheep back on his shoulders, but the shepherd rejoices. Similarly, God has more intense happiness at the return of a sinner than at people who are righteous. This parable is another attempt to make the Pharisees see others, particularly sinners, in a different light. Jesus does not condemn sinners, but lovingly works for their well-being. He says, "Those who are well do not need a physician, but the sick do. I did not come to call the righteous, but sinners" (Matthew 9:12-13).

POINTS FOR DISCUSSION
• Signs that the one sheep is very precious to the shepherd

• The value of each individual person
• How the lost sheep feels
• Why we should not fear the sacrament of reconciliation
• How we regard sinners
• Ways we shepherd one another

THE LOST COIN

Luke 15:8-10
Twenty-Fourth Sunday of the Year C

Cast	*Props*
Jesus	Ten silver coins
Mary	Candle with paper
James	flame
Sarah	Broom
Rachel	Pot and ladle
Woman	Table
Neighbors +	

THEMES
Forgiveness of sin,
sacrament of reconciliation

COMMENTS
The parable is one of the simplest. The setting of the story is a house, and the main character is a housewife. Homely as it is, it turns the Pharisees' concept of God upside-down. In the first place God is compared to a woman. Secondly, the common experience of looking for a lost object and finding it is used to explain God's attitude toward sinners.

The lost coin has some special meaning for the woman. Scholars suggest that it was one of the coins that were her personal property worn in her headdress or necklace and marking her as a married woman. In any case, she desperately searches her house and holds a celebration when she finds the coin. The parable implies that sinners catapult God into the same frustration and distress that the missing coin causes the woman. God takes the initiative in seeking out the lost. Once they are recovered, all heaven rejoices. This picture of a God who is loving and compassionate toward sinners is quite new to those Pharisees who are righteous and rigid.

POINTS FOR DISCUSSION

- Personal experiences of losing and finding something precious
- Images of God
- The beauty of the sacrament of reconciliation
- Groups of sinners that we have a hard time loving
- Ways we can reach out to the sinner

THE PRODIGAL SON

Luke 15:11-32
Fourth Sunday of Lent C
Twenty-Fourth Sunday of the Year C

CAST	PROPS
Jesus	Two scrolls of paper
Father	Bag of money
Younger Son	Sack of corn
Older Son	Robe
Neighbor	Ring
Employer	Shoes
Servants 1, 2	Music

THEMES

Forgiveness, sacrament of reconciliation, righteousness

COMMENTS

This parable might more aptly be named the forgiving father. The hero of the story is the father of two sons who is indulgent, generous, and forgiving. He exhibits an unconditional love that embraces both his weak, foolish son and his resentful, obedient son. The father is a reflection of God who does more than tolerate our foolishness. God longs for us to come to our senses and to trust his love enough to go to him in our need.

The younger son wastes his inheritance and ends up feeding pigs, the lowest job for a Jewish person, and one that cuts him off from his people. He decides to apply for a job at home as a hired servant, the lowliest type of servant. The father must have been looking for his son. When he sees him, he runs to him, something beneath the dignity of a Near Eastern man. For a welcome the father offers no lecture, no punishment—just a hug, reinstatement as a son, and a celebration. The older boy, sulking because of the father's loving reception of the returned scoundrel, represents those righteous ones who begrudge others God's mercy.

POINTS FOR DISCUSSION

- The callousness and foolishness of the younger son
- Signs of the father's love
- The surprising image of God
- Whether or not the older son went to the celebration in the end
- Why we should go to God after we sin

- How we should feel toward other sinners
- Which character of the story we best identify with

- Why God doesn' t punish all evil people on earth
- How sinners can be helped to conversion
- The Christian attitude toward sinners
- The explanation of the parable given in Matthew 13:36-43

THE WEEDS

Matthew 13:24-30
Sixteenth Sunday of the Year A

CAST	PROPS
Jesus	Two baskets
Sower	
Enemy	
Servants 1, 2	

THEME
Evil

COMMENTS
This parable, along with the parables of the Mustard Seed and the Leaven, is known as the Great Assurance. It occurs after accounts of some Pharisees' attacks on Jesus. Through parables Jesus explains how the kingdom of God will be spread through the world gradually. In this parable, the weeds sown by the enemy were darnel, a type of weed that resembles wheat in its early stages. Jesus explains that good people, children of God, and sinners, children of Satan, live together on earth. The separation of good and evil will not occur until the end of the world. Even Jesus associates with tax collectors and sinners. His disciples then should not exclude sinners from their ministry or judge them. At the final coming Jesus will separate the unrepentant from the saints.

THE HIDDEN TREASURE

Matthew 13:44
Seventeenth Sunday of the Year A

CAST	PROPS
Jesus	Treasure chest
Man	Paper dirt
Buyers 1, 2, 3	Coins
Owner	

THEME
Value of the kingdom

COMMENTS
This parable focuses on the great joy of the person who comes upon the reign of God. It is compared to the joy of someone who unexpectedly finds a treasure. In Palestine, at that time, people kept their valuables safe by burying them in the ground. In the parable the man who discovers the treasure has a legal right to it, if the land is his. He prizes the treasure so much that he is willing to trade everything he owns to possess it. Similarly, people who understand the value of the kingdom of heaven gladly give up everything to possess it. They strive for this magnificent goal with

eager determination, although in the eyes of the world they may be considered reckless or foolish.

POINTS FOR DISCUSSION
• Experiences that bring great joy
• How we first come to find the kingdom
• Times when we've had a foretaste of the peace, joy, and love that characterize the kingdom
• What we might have to give up for the sake of the reign of God
• How chances to possess the kingdom can be lost by not seizing the moment
• Examples of people who have sacrificed earthly goods for heaven

large and lovely pearl. He doesn't just stumble over it, as the man who found the treasure in the field. Finally, the merchant's efforts are rewarded. He recognizes a priceless pearl and sells all he has to possess it. Heaven is like this pearl. Those who realize its true value will do anything to obtain it. No matter how high the price, it is always a bargain.

POINTS FOR DISCUSSION
• The joys of heaven
• Why people don' t always recognize the value of heaven
• Other "pearls" people are willing to sacrifice for
• Some hard things that God asks of us

THE PEARL OF GREAT PRICE

Matthew 13:45-46
Seventeenth Sunday of the Year A

CAST	PROPS
Jesus	Desk for Salesman
Man	Beads or marbles for
Salesman	pearls, one larger
	than others
	Coins

THEMES
Value of the kingdom, materialism

COMMENTS
The supereme worth of the kingdom of heaven is taught by the story of a purchase. To the Jewish people a pearl was the most precious jewel. In the parable a pearl merchant searches for an exceptionally

THE GREAT BANQUET

Luke 14:16-24

CAST

Jesus
Master
Poor Couple
Servant
Crippled Woman
Blind Man
Guests 1, 2, 3
Other Guests +

THEME
Members of the kingdom

COMMENTS
Jesus is dining at the home of a leading Pharisee. When someone remarks, "Blessed is the one who will dine in the kingdom of

kingdom of God," Jesus responds with the parable of the great banquet. Obviously the banquet represents the kingdom of heaven and the host, God.

During the time of Jesus people received two invitations to feasts: Those who said yes to the first one were invited again when everything was ready. In the parable the first guests invited are very rude. Not only do they fail to keep their first commitment, but their excuses are ridiculous. These guests are like the people of Israel who refused Jesus' invitation to the kingdom.

The second group in the parable, the beggars and outcasts of society, are the sinners who recognize their need for salvation. The third group of guests are hoboes and strangers on the roads outside the city walls. They are the Gentiles. In essence, Jesus reveals that everyone is invited to the kingdom of heaven.

POINTS FOR DISCUSSION
• Why Jesus chooses to compare God's kingdom to a banquet
• The kind of host God is described as
• How we accept God's invitation
• How we reject it
• Lame excuses we give for not trying to get into God's kingdom by honoring God, living justly, obeying authority, respecting life, etc.

THE WICKED VINEDRESSERS

Matthew 21:33-41   Mark 12:1-12
Luke 20:9-16
Twenty-Seventh Sunday of the Year A

CAST

Jesus
Landowner
Tenants 1, 2
Servants 1, 2, 3, 4
Son

THEME
Virtue

COMMENTS
Vineyards were a familiar sight on the hillsides of Israel. Jesus knew how they were protected by walls and watchtowers. He knew about the winepress, rocks on which the grapes were squeezed to yield the juice that would become wine. Already in Isaiah, chapter 5 a vineyard stands for the House of Israel. In Jesus' parable, the history of Israel is presented. The man who plants a vineyard represents God who carefully tended the people Israel. Just as the tenants do not hand over the produce to the servants, the leaders did not yield good works at the prophets' pleadings.

The tenants in the parable throw the son out of the vineyard and kill him because by Jewish law if a man had no heirs his property went to his tenants. Tradition holds that Jesus, the Son of God, was killed outside the city walls of Jerusalem. In telling the story the "son," Jesus announces, to the "tenants" that God will give the kingdom of heaven to a new people: believers, whether Israelites or Gentiles.

The king's lack of retaliation mirrors God's goodness in dealing with us.

POINTS FOR DISCUSSION
- How much God loved the vineyard Israel
- How the parable compares to Jesus' life
- What harvest we are expected to produce
- Prophets who speak to us

THE WORKERS IN THE VINEYARD

Matthew 20:1-16
Twenty-Fifth Sunday of the Year A

CAST	PROPS
Jesus	Five baskets for
Employer	grapes
First Workers 1, 2	Ten silver coins
Second Workers 1, 2	
Third Workers 1, 2	
Fourth Workers 1, 2	
Last Workers 1, 2	
Foreman	

THEME
Members of the kingdom

COMMENTS
At first glance the employer in this parable might seem unjust, or at least a bit crazy. Actually he is just very benevolent. The focus of the parable is the employer who rewards all his workers equally—even those who come at the last minute. With incredible loving mercy God grants heaven to people who repent late in life as well as people who have been faithful all their lives. God is free to do this.

The Law of Moses stipulated that day laborers were to be paid before sundown. Holy people who resent the good fortune of repentant sinners the way the first workers did the generous pay of the last workers are not so holy after all. Law-conscious Jewish Christians needed this lesson in regard to sinners and Gentiles who joined the church of Jesus.

POINTS FOR DISCUSSION
- How I would feel if I were a first worker, a last worker, the employer
- Ways God shows kindness to all
- How some "lasts" might be discovered "firsts" in the kingdom of God
- Examples illustrating the free gift of grace

THE WEDDING FEAST

Matthew 22:1-14
Twenty-Eighth Sunday of Year A

CAST	PROPS
Jesus	Old shirt or jacket
King	for wedding guest
Servants 1, 2, 3, 4	
Guests 1, 2, 3, 4	
Persons 1, 2, 3 +	
Man	

THEMES
Members of the kingdom, readiness for the kingdom

COMMENTS
In the ancient Near East the initial invitation was followed by a second invitation immediately before the celebration. To refuse to go to the feast after first accepting

was the height of discourtesy. Since going to a feast for a king's son was a chance to pay homage, the refusal in this parable was also insulting on the political level.

The wedding feast is a symbol of heaven. This parable shows how Israel, the chosen people, sometimes rejected salvation and even killed the prophets who invited them to it. All people are welcome then. But the man who came later without a wedding garment, a clean white robe, was also rude, especially if, as some scholars think, wedding clothes were provided at the feast. Through laziness or pride he did not put one on. Similarly, we can only enjoy the eternal feast if we are clothed with good deeds. We, too, might miss salvation.

The building of the city in the parable may have been added as a reference to the destruction of Jerusalem in AD 70.

POINTS FOR DISCUSSION

- How to obtain a wedding garment
- How we received the invitation to salvation
- If the wedding garment is the life we received at baptism, how it can be lost
- Appreciation for the gift of salvation
- The necessity of cooperating with the graces of salvation

A HOUSE BUILT ON ROCK

Matthew 7:24-27   Luke 6:47-49
Ninth Sunday of the Year A

CAST	PROPS
Jesus	Two chairs
Man 1, 2	Sound effects for storm and collapse of house

THEME
Hearing God's word

COMMENTS
Jesus draws on his experience as a craftsman to teach a lesson on listening to God's word. He knew that a house built on a rock foundation is more secure than one resting on sand. God's word is as strong and bracing as solid rock. A person who acts on it can weather all storms. In contrast, a person who chooses not to live according to God's words eventually finds his or her life a shambles. Wise persons heed God's words; fools ignore them. Wise persons plan for the future; fools live only for the day.

POINTS FOR DISCUSSION

- The characteristics of sand and sand castles
- Ways we receive the message of God's word
- Some words of God that lead to a successful life
- What the storm stands for
- Examples of how not acting on God's word can have harmful consequences
- The difficulty of building on rock: why acting on God's words demands more of us
- Favorite words of God

THE SOWER

Matthew 13:3-9, 18-23   Mark 4:2-9, 14-20, Luke 8:4-8, 11-15
Fifteenth Sunday of the Year A

CAST	PROPS
Jesus	Flashlight for sun
Farmer	Nineteen paper ears
Two Seeds for path	of corn
Two Seeds for rocks	Basket
Two Seeds for thorns	
Three good Seeds	
Two birds	
Two thorns	
Sun	
Crowd +	

THEME
Hearing God's word

COMMENTS
Coming from Galilee, a highly agricultural society, Jesus finds in a sower and seed a natural image of God and God's word. In those days farmers planted seeds by casting huge quantities on the ground and then plowing. Footpaths ran through the fields, and slabs of limestone lay close to the surface in some areas. The fate of seeds in different environments correspond to the fate of God's words in people's lives. In some people the word never has a chance at all. It is immediately destroyed. In stone-hearted people, it does not take root and withers at the first challenge. Sometimes the word is choked by life's cares, activities, and pleasures. But some people are like rich soil where the seed produces a great harvest. In the parable much seed is wasted, but what does grow produces a great amount. The reign of God will prevail, despite obstacles.

POINTS FOR DISCUSSION
• The types of hearts God's word falls on
• Where we receive God's word
• How to make ourselves good soil
• Examples of "words" we should take to heart
• What the harvest is
• Why God's word is rejected today

THE GOOD SAMARITAN

Luke 10:25-37
Fifteenth Sunday of the Year C

CAST	PROPS
Jesus	Wallet
Crowd +	Two silver pieces
Teacher of the Law	Two jars for oil
Man	and wine
Samaritan	White cloth for
Robbers 1, 2	bandage
Priest	
Levite	
Innkeeper	

THEME
Love of neighbor, prejudice

COMMENTS
This classic story of human mercy is actually Jesus' commentary on the law. The Teacher of the law correctly identifies the path to eternal life as the two greatest commandments: love of God (in the words of the shema, the Jewish prayer prayed twice a day) and love of neighbor. Jesus illustrates the preeminence of love by a story about a person whose love is stronger than religious taboos, prejudices, and con-

cern for self. The priest and Levite do not assist the victim perhaps because contact with him would make them unclean, and they would not be able to perform their functions at the temple. Perhaps they thought the man was a decoy for bandits who worked the dangerous route. In any case, the priest and Levite avoid carrying out God's law.

In contrast, the Samaritan, even though he belongs to a people considered impure—traitors and heretics—ministers to the man in need. Moreover, he does so with unusual generosity, sacrificing his time, his goods, his money, and a night's sleep. Besides teaching that love is superior to legalism, Jesus' parable teaches that love must be practical, manifested in deeds. Furthermore, the Good Samaritan story clarifies that the neighbor we are to love is everyone, including our enemies.

POINTS FOR DISCUSSION
- The use of the phrase "good samaritan" today
- People comparable to the Samaritans for us
- Reasons why the priest and Levite do not help the victim
- The thoughts and feelings of the victim when he realized it was a Samaritan who saved his life
- What happened next
- Excuses we can give for not performing acts of kindness
- Sacrifices that love demands

THE PERSISTENT FRIEND

Luke 11:5-8
Seventeenth Sunday of the Year C

CAST	PROPS
Jesus	Mat or carpeting
Disciples +	for bed
Sam	Chair
Traveler	Three loaves of bread
Friend	
Children 1, 2 +	

THEME
Perseverance in prayer

COMMENTS
The Jewish people considered hospitality a sacred duty. The man in this parable was bound to serve his unexpected guest. When he disturbs his neighbor for help, not only is it in the middle of the night, but to open the door the friend has to remove a heavy wooden or iron bar. No doubt the whole family was awakened since they all slept on the floor of the small house. Nevertheless, the neighbor responds to the man's pleas because of his friend's persistence. This is a lesson in perseverance in prayer. Of course, God, who is more than friend to us, will answer our cries for help. As a loving parent, God is at our service any time. All we have to do is trust and knock.

POINTS FOR DISCUSSION
- Our feelings on being disturbed during the night
- How God feels when we keep asking for something
- God's desire for us to pray
- When we should pray

- How God answers our prayers
- What might keep us from praying

THE RICH FOOL

||||||||||||||||||||||||||||||||||||||||||||||||||||||||||||||||||||||||||

Luke 12:16-21
Eighteenth Sunday of the Year C

CAST

Jesus
Rich Man
Servant
Voice of God

THEMES
Materialism, readiness for the kingdom, riches

COMMENTS
Jesus puts this world's goods in proper perspective in this story. As the rich man solves his problem, his thoughts center around "I." He seems to have forgotten about God and his neighbor as he plans for the future. He has a rude awakening. Unfortunately, he hasn't planned for the ultimate future and faces judgment unprepared. The money and property we accumulate in this life mean nothing when we die. In the words of a Spanish proverb: "There are no pockets in shrouds." On the other hand, we will have to give an account of our spiritual wealth. Those who spend their life seeking natural goods rather than spiritual goods will someday regret their mistaken values. As Jesus asks, "What good is it if a person gains the whole world but loses life?" (Matthew 16:26)

POINTS FOR DISCUSSION
- Why the man in the parable was a fool
- Signs of materialism today
- Sharing the goods of the earth
- How to grow rich spiritually
- The unpredictability of death

THE BARREN FIG TREE

||||||||||||||||||||||||||||||||||||||||||||||||||||||||||||||||||||||||||||||||||||||

Luke 13:6-9
Third Sunday of the Year C

CAST	*PROPS*
Jesus	Tree (a plant or a
Man	drawing on the
Gardener	board)

THEMES
Good deeds, use of gifts, virtue

COMMENTS
In this parable Jesus draws a comparison from nature to encourage his followers to put their faith into action. Just as a fig tree is expected to yield fruit, we sons and daughters of God are expected to produce good deeds. Ordinarily a fig tree needs no extra care. The gardener takes unusual measures to get the barren tree to bear fruit. He does not give up on it. Similarly God endeavors to cultivate virtue in us through grace. Although God is patient, eventually people who do not act like the holy children of God they were meant to be will be deprived of eternal life.

- What figs are
- How it would feel to plant and care for an orange tree or a walnut tree that never bore fruit
- Kinds of fruit we are to produce
- Helps God gives us to bear good fruit

THE CRAFTY STEWARD

Luke 16:1-9
Twenty-Fifth Sunday of the Year C

CAST	PROPS
Jesus	Two scrolls for
Rich Man	invoices
Reporter	Desk and chair
Steward	
Messenger	
Debtors 1, 2	

THEMES
Discipleship, use of gifts

COMMENTS
A steward in charge of finances is about to be fired for squandering his employer's money. As preparation for the future when he will need friends, the shrewd agent does a favor for his employer's debtors: He reduces the amount they owe. The steward is praised not for his crooked acts, but for his ingenuity in managing his life. This parable concretizes Jesus' advice to his disciples, "Be shrewd as serpents and simple as doves" (Matthew 10:11).

The war between good and evil demands clever strategies on our part. It may even require sacrificing material goods. If peo-ple in the business world apply themselves earnestly to gain material goods, shouldn't we devote our energy and intelligence to working for heavenly goods?

POINTS FOR DISCUSSION

- How the parable teaches at the outset that crime does not pay
- What the steward did to make the debtors happy
- The reason why the rich man praised the steward
- How to be clever in fighting evil in specific cases
- Instances where sacrificing something new leads to better things in the future
- A comparison of the efforts we make to live our beliefs, and the efforts we make to earn money, look good, be entertained, etc.

THE RICH MAN AND LAZARUS

Luke 16:19-31
Twenty-Sixth Sunday of the Year C

CAST	PROPS
Jesus	Plate, cup
Rich Man	Desk for table
Lazarus	
Servant	
Abraham	
Angels +	

THEMES

Hearing God's word, love of neighbor, materialism, riches, virtue

COMMENTS

This parable in Luke is the story form of a beatitude of the Sermon on the Plain (6:20-26). Those who are hungry now will be satisfied, and those who are filled now will be hungry. The rich man and Lazarus are at extreme ends of the economic scale. The rich man wears purple robes and linen undergarments, the clothes of the elite, while Lazarus longs for even the scraps from the table. Someone suggests that these scraps are hunks of bread that the diners, who have no silverware, use to wipe their fingers.

Being rich is no sin, but the selfish use of riches is. The rich man's crime is that he ignores the human being in need on his doorstep. He gets his just deserts in hell, while Lazarus rests with Abraham, which meant the highest level of bliss. When the rich man tries to prevent his brothers from repeating his mistake, he is told that they have had enough warning. Abraham's ending statement is prophetic. Although Jesus did rise from the dead, people continue in their selfish, uncaring ways.

POINTS FOR DISCUSSION

- The identity of Abraham as the first believer
- Who the poor are in our lives and how we can help them
- The finality of death and the afterlife
- Jesus' other teachings about riches
- Being aware of other's needs

THE JUDGE AND THE WIDOW

Luke 18:1-8
Twenty-Ninth Sunday of the Year C

CAST

Jesus
Judge
Widow
Person
Visitor

THEME

Perseverance in prayer

COMMENTS

On the natural plane, even a rock-like resistance is eroded by constant pounding. Jesus illustrates this by the story of a woman who hounds a tough, unjust judge for her rights. Weary of her persistent nagging, the judge finally agrees to use his power to give her what she wants. Jesus assures us that in the same way God will respond to our cries for justice. Not a grasping, selfish judge, but a generous Father, God hears us when we call. With confidence, trust, and patience we can turn to the Lord, our just and merciful judge, for help. If we never give up asking, God will reward us with the good we desire.

POINTS FOR DISCUSSION
- The reason the judge relented
- Things that are worth praying for
- Stories of prayers that were eventually answered
- Ways of praying repeatedly for something
- Other advice Jesus gives about prayer
- Why God answers our prayers
- The similarity of the proverb "The squeaking wheel gets the oil"

THE PHARISEE AND THE TAX COLLECTOR

Luke 18:9-14
Twentieth Sunday of the Year C

CAST
Jesus
Pharisee
Tax Collector
Crowd +

THEMES
Self-righteousness, humility, virtue

COMMENTS
A Pharisee, an expert in religion, was meticulous in keeping the laws. On the other hand, a tax collector had the reputation of being dishonest. Tax collectors in Palestine were despised because they collected money for Rome, the oppressor, and pocketed whatever was above their quota.

Through two brief prayers Jesus sketches the pictures of a proud, holy man and a humble sinner. This self-righteous Pharisee's prayer is a list of his own accomplishments. Although he may have done more than required in fasting and tithing, he gives the impression that he has earned God's love. On the other hand, the tax collector's prayer is an admission of guilt and a plea for help. In fact, he calls himself "*the* sinner." This Pharisee has done everything perfectly, but he is obnoxious in his smugness. The tax collector, relying on God for salvation rather than himself, is a better candidate for sainthood.

POINTS FOR DISCUSSION
- Why the tax collector was more pleasing to God
- The good that the Pharisee has done and the faults that spoil it
- The role of God in our salvation compared to our own role
- What it means to be humble
- Samples of other prayers that acknowledge our dependence on God
- Biblical or contemporary examples of humble people who have been exalted and proud people who have been humbled

THE UNFORGIVING SERVANT

||||||||||||||||||||||||||||||||||||||||||||||||||||||||||||||||||||||||||||||||

Matthew 18:21-35
Twenty-Fourth Sunday of the Year A

CAST	PROPS
Jesus	A scroll
Peter	
King	
Servants 1, 2, 3, 4	

THEMES
Forgiveness, sacrament of reconciliation, virtue

COMMENTS
Jesus' disciples should be distinguished by their readiness to forgive one another. The Lord's Prayer reminds us of this when we pray "Forgive us our trespasses as we forgive those who trespass against us." Through the parable of the unforgiving servant, we come to realize that mercy toward others is a logical response since God has forgiven us what we could never make up for.

In those days it was the practice of higher servants to borrow their rich employer's money for private investments of their own. The servant in the parable owed the king an exorbitant amount of money, which he could never repay. The oriental king unexpectedly waived the entire debt for his servant. Then when this servant met someone who owed him only a paltry sum, he dared to treat him harshly for not being able to repay him. The servant's action is obviously outrageous. The parable makes plain why we ought to be willing to forgive our brothers and sisters seventy-seven times, which means an indefinite number of times.

POINTS FOR DISCUSSION
- The seriousness of our offenses against God
- Ways to express gratitude to God for forgiving us
- When we might have to forgive people
- How forgiveness is shown

THE TWO SONS

||||||||||||||||||||||||||||||||||||||||||||||||||||||||||||||||||||||||||||||||

Matthew 21:28-32
Twenty-Sixth Sunday of the Year A

CAST
Jesus
Religious Leaders +
Father
Sons 1, 2

THEME
Virtue

COMMENTS
On one level this parable instructs us to act according to our words. Mere lip service is worthless. If we say we are Christians, our lives should show it. We should not be like the older son who says one thing and does another. Better to be like the younger son who has a change of heart and carries out the father's will after all. On another level, since Jesus is speaking to the chief priests and elders, this parable is seen as a condemnation of them. The older son represents the religious leaders. They originally bound themselves to follow God's law as the chosen people, but then did not accept the prophet John and Jesus. The younger son stands for the religious out-

casts who repented and the Gentiles who received salvation. Someone once pointed out that Jesus is the third son who said yes and lived yes.

POINTS FOR DISCUSSION
- The importance of keeping promises and resolutions
- Responsibilities our baptismal commitment entails
- The constant opportunity for conversion
- How we say yes by our actions

THE TEN BRIDESMAIDS
||||||||||||||||||||||||||||||||||||||||||||||||||||||||||||||||||||||||||||
Matthew 25:1-13
Thirty-Second Sunday of the Year A

CAST	PROPS
Jesus	Ten lamps
Wise Brides-maids 1, 2, 3, 4, 5	five with large flames, five with small flames
Foolish Brides-maids 1, 2, 3, 4, 5	Five containers of oil
Bridegroom	
Announcer	
Servant	
Crowd +	

THEMES
Good deeds, readiness for the kingdom

COMMENTS
This is one of the crisis parables that show how we must act immediately to choose salvation. Through lack of planning and foresight, the five foolish bridesmaids miss the wedding feast. Jesus wants us to be prepared with good deeds since we do not

know when the kingdom will come. Just as the bridegroom in the parable did not come on schedule, the kingdom did not arrive when the Israelites had expected. Now two thousand years later, we still await it. When the divine bridegroom arrives to take us into the eternal feast, we should be ready with our lamps burning brightly. Those who are not caught by surprise will be admitted to the joys of heaven.

POINTS FOR DISCUSSION
- The fault of the foolish bridesmaids and the consequences
- What oil we should have ready
- How to make sure the bridegroom recognizes us
- The unpredictability of our own death and the end of the world

THE THREE SERVANTS AND THE MONEY
||||||||||||||||||||||||||||||||||||||||||||||||||||||||||||||||||||||||||||
Matthew 25:14-30 Luke 19:11-27
Thirty-Third Sunday of the Year A

CAST	PROPS
Jesus	Five bags of money:
Crowd +	2 marked 5000,
Man	2 marked 2000,
Servants 1, 2, 3	1 marked 1000
Banker	Shovel
	"Bank" sign

THEMES
Good deeds, use of gifts

COMMENTS
This parable illustrates the necessity of us-

ing whatever gifts we have been given—both spiritual and natural gifts. Two servants put their money to work and increase it. They are handsomely rewarded. The third servant does absolutely nothing with the money entrusted to him. He doesn't even put it in the bank. For his lack of initiative he is severely punished. Our sharing of the master's joy depends on our response to his graces and gifts. We can either develop our gifts and share them, or we can bury them and waste them. The choice is ours. The parable can also be taken as a warning to some Pharisees who wanted to keep things as they were.

POINTS FOR DISCUSSION

- Kinds of gifts we are given and how they can be used
- What our master expects of us
- Gifts that disappear through lack of use
- Why we fear using gifts
- Examples of people who are using their gifts
- The meaning of the saying, "What I am is God's gift to me; what I become is my gift to God."
- The fate of useless servants now and later

SUNDAY GOSPELS
CONTAINING MIRACLES OR PARABLES

Playlets can help prepare the students to celebrate Sunday liturgies. The Gospels of the following Sundays are about a miracle or a parable.

SUNDAY LITURGY	MIRACLE / PARABLE
Third Sunday of Lent C	The Barren Fig Tree
Fourth Sunday of Lent A	The Man Born Blind
Fourth Sunday of Lent C	The Prodigal Son
Fifth Sunday of Lent A	The Raising of Lazarus
Third Sunday of Easter C	The Second Large Catch of Fish
Second Sunday of the Year C	Water into Wine
Fourth Sunday of the Year B	A Possessed Man
Fifth Sunday of the Year B	Peter's Mother-in-Law
Fifth Sunday of the Year C	The Large Catch of Fish
Sixth Sunday of the Year B	A Leper
Seventh Sunday of the Year B	The Paralytic
Ninth Sunday of the Year A	A House Built on Rock
Ninth Sunday of the Year B	The Man with a Withered Hand
Ninth Sunday of the Year C	The Centurion's Servant
Tenth Sunday of the Year C	Raising the Widow's Son
Twelfth Sunday of the Year B	The Calming of the Storm
Thirteenth Sunday of the Year B	Raising Jairus's Daughter and Healing the Sick Woman
Fifteenth Sunday of the Year A	The Sower
Fifteenth Sunday of the Year C	The Good Samaritan
Sixteenth Sunday of the Year A	The Weeds
Seventeenth Sunday of the Year A	The Hidden Treasure The Pearl of Great Price
Seventeenth Sunday of the Year B	Multiplication of Loaves
Seventeenth Sunday of the Year C	The Persistent Friend
Eighteenth Sunday of the Year A	The Multiplication of Loaves
Eighteenth Sunday of the Year C	The Rich Fool
Nineteenth Sunday of the Year A	Walking on the Sea
Twentieth Sunday of the Year A	The Canaanite Woman

Twenty-Third Sunday of the Year B	Cure of a Deaf Mute
Twenty-Fourth Sunday of the Year A	The Unforgiving Servant
Twenty-Fourth Sunday of the Year C	The Lost Sheep
	The Lost Coin
	The Prodigal Son
Twenty-Fifth Sunday of the Year A	The Workers in the Vineyard
Twenty-Fifth Sunday of the Year C	The Crafty Steward
Twenty-Sixth Sunday of the Year A	The Two Sons
Twenty-Sixth Sunday of the Year C	The Rich Man and Lazarus
Twenty-Seventh Sunday of the Year A	The Wicked Vinedressers
Twenty-Eighth Sunday of the Year A	The Wedding Feast
Twenty-Eighth Sunday of the Year C	The Ten Lepers
Twenty-Ninth Sunday of the Year C	The Judge and the Widow
Thirtieth Sunday of the Year B	Blind Bartimaeus
Thirtieth Sunday of the Year C	The Pharisee and the Tax Collector
Thirty-Second Sunday of the Year A	The Ten Bridesmaids
Thirty-Third Sunday of the Year A	The Three Servants and the Money

INDEX OF THEMES

The following topics can be enlivened by a playlet about a miracle or parable.

SELECTED BIBLIOGRAPHY

MIRACLES

Allen, Ronald. *Our Eyes Can Be Opened.* Latham, Maryland: University Press of America, 1982.

Barclay, William. *And He Had Compassion: The Healing Miracles of Jesus.* Valley Forge: Judson Press, 1976.

Borsch, Frederick. *Power in Weakness: New Hearings for Gospel Stories.* Philadelphia: Fortress Press, 1983.

Fuller, R. *Interpreting the Miracles.* Philadelphia: Westminster Press, 1963.

Kee, H.C. *Miracles in the Early Christian World.* New Haven: Yale University Press, 1983.

Lewis, C.S. *Miracles: A Preliminary Study.* New York: Macmillan, 1947.

McInerny, Ralph M. *Miracles: A Catholic View.* Huntington, Indiana: Our Sunday Visitor, 1986.

Moule, Charles Francis Digby. *Miracles.* ed. by C.F.D. Moule. London: A. R. Mowbray and Company, 1965.

Richards, H.J. *The Miracles of Jesus: What Really Happened?* Mystic, Connecticut: Twenty-Third Publications, 1986.

Theissen, G. *Miracle Stories of the Early Christian Tradition.* ed. John Riches. Philadelphia: Fortress Press, 1983.

van der Loos, H. *The Miracles of Jesus.* Leiden: Brill, 1975.

PARABLES

Armstrong, April Oursler. *The Tales Christ Told.* New York: Doubleday, 1959.

Armstrong, Edward. *The Gospel Parables.* New York: Sheed and Ward, 1967.

Barclay, William. *And Jesus Said.* Philadelphia: The Westminster Press, 1970.

Dodd, C. H. *The Parables of the Kingdom.* New York: Charles Scribner's Sons, 1961.

Fonck, Leopold, S.J. *The Parables of the Gospel.* New York: Frederick Prestet Company, 1914.

Hendrickx, Herman. *The Parables of Jesus: Studies in the Synoptic Gospels.* San Francisco: Harper & Row, 1987.

Jeremias, Joachim. *The Parables of Jesus.* New York: Charles Scribner's Sons, 1972.

_____. *Rediscovering the Parables.* New York: Charles Scribner's Sons, 1966.

Kistemaker. *The Parables of Jesus.* Grand Rapids: Baker Book House, 1980.

Lowery, Daniel, C.Ss.R. *The Parables of Jesus.* Liguori, Missouri: Liguori Publications, 1987. Perkins, Pheme. *Hearing the Parables of Jesus.* New York: Paulist Press, 1981.

More Books By Sister Kathleen...

Leading Students Into Prayer
Ideas and Suggestions from A to Z
The author explores the varied forms that prayer can take for children: personal and communal, vocal and mental, liturgical, Scripture-based, centering, and traditional. Any teacher with a personal copy of this treasure-store of prayer activities and techniques will have many exciting ideas to incorporate into religion lessons, as well as for personal inspiration and practice.

ISBN: 0-89622-549-6, 160 pp, $12.95 (order W-68)

Leading Students into Scripture
Here are dozens of easy-to-imitate techniques to help students know and love the Bible. Most of the successfully-used methods can be adapted for different grade levels.

ISBN: 0-89622-328-0, 112 pp, $9.95 (order W-18)

Discipline Made Easy
Positive Tips and Techniques for Religion Teachers
Joe Paprocki says he has been looking for a book like this ever since he became a DRE. The author provides hundreds of tested techniques to provide encouragement for volunteer catechists and wise insighs for veterans. ISBN: 0-89622-598-4, 112 pp, 7.95 (order W–46)

Weekday Liturgies with Children
Creative Ways to Celebrate Year-Round
Sr. Kathleen provides guidelines and suggestions for making liturgies more interesting and appealing to children while involving them in the celebration. Her book includes themes, suggestions for intercessions, homily guidelines, and many ways to vary the singing, prayers, and other parts of the Mass.

ISBN: 0-89622-694-8, 248 pp, $29.95 (order M-74)

Available at religious bookstores or from:

TWENTY-THIRD PUBLICATIONS
P.O. Box 180 • Mystic, CT 06355

For a complete list of quality books and videos call:
1 - 8 0 0 - 3 2 1 - 0 4 1 1